BERT MEYERS

On the Life and Work of an American Master

Bert Meyers: On the Life & Work of an American Master

ISBN: 978-1-7344356-3-4

Published by Unsung Masters Series in collaboration with *Gulf Coast, Copper Nickel,* and *Pleiades.*

Department of English
University of Houston
Houston, TX 77204

Produced at the University of Houston Department of English

Distributed by Small Press Distribution (SPD) and to subscribers of *Copper Nickel, Pleiades: Literature in Context* and *Gulf Coast: A Journal of Literature and Fine Arts.*

Series, cover, and interior design by Martin Rock.
Cover photograph by Elliott Erwitt, courtesty of Daniel Meyers.

2 4 6 8 9 7 5 3 1
First Printing, 2023

The Unsung Masters Series brings the work of great, out-of-print, little-known writers to new readers. Each volume in the Series includes a large selection of the author's original writing, as well as essays on the writer, interviews with people who knew the writer, photographs, and ephemera. The curators of the Unsung Masters Series are always interested in suggestions for future volumes.

Invaluable financial support for this project
has been provided by the Nancy Luton Fund
and the University of Houston English Department.

UNIVERSITY of **HOUSTON**

BERT MEYERS

On the Life and Work of an American Master

Edited by DANA LEVIN
and ADELE ELISE WILLIAMS

RECENT BOOKS IN THE UNSUNG MASTERS SERIES

2022

Jean Ross Justice: On the Life and Work of an American Master
Edited by Ryan Bollenbach & Kevin Prufer

2021

Shreela Ray: On the Life and Work of an American Master
Edited by Kazim Ali & Rohan Chhetri

2020

Wendy Battin: On the Life and Work of an American Master
Edited by Charles Hartman, Martha Collins, Pamela Alexander, & Matthew Krajniak

2019

Laura Hershey: On the Life & Work of an American Master
Edited by Meg Day & Niki Herd

2018

Adelaide Crapsey: On the Life and Work of an American Master
Edited by Jenny Molberg & Christian Bancroft

2017

Belle Turnbull: On the Life & Work of an American Master
Edited by David Rothman & Jeffrey Villines

2016

Beatrice Hastings: On the Life & Work of Modern Master
Edited by Benjamin Johnson & Erika Jo Brown

2015

Catherine Breese Davis: On the Life & Work of an American Master
Edited by Martha Collins, Kevin Prufer, & Martin Rock

THE UNSUNG MASTERS SERIES

IN COLLABORATION WITH

PLEIADES
PRESS

CONTENTS

INTRODUCTION

BEGINNINGS

THE WORK

POSTSCRIPTS

INDICES AND CREDITS

INTRODUCTION

ON BERT MEYERS

Dana Levin

As an undergraduate at Pitzer College in 1984, I set up camp in the Bert Meyers Poetry Room. It was upstairs in the front bedroom of the Grove House, a Craftsman style bungalow that had been moved to campus with great fanfare some years before to serve as a student union of sorts. For three years, I read and wrote under the gaze of a portrait of Bert, which had a knack for falling off the wall with a crash whenever I was especially brooding about life—what a startle! At those moments I always thought Bert was trying to get my attention: "Snap out of it! Get back to work!" And so I would. I hung out in the Poetry Room so much I moved in by accretion, eventually spending each night on the outside sleeping porch just off a side window for most of a semester, until the custodial staff found me out. Although Bert was five years dead when I started college, his presence was very alive in that room and in the classrooms where I began to study poetry.

I was introduced to his work by his former students, taught his work by his former colleagues, immersed myself in it in a room that housed his library of beat-up paperbacks. As someone who showed up to college in love with the poems of T.S. Eliot, I found books and periodicals among Bert's collection that blew my mind open to contemporary poetry in English. Ntozake Shange's *Nappy Edges* and Galway Kinnell's *The Book of Nightmares* left indelible marks, as did many poems in translation—by Julio Cortázar, Antonio Machado, Paul Celan—which I found in well-worn issues of Robert Bly's influential magazine, *The Sixties*. Even in death, Bert was teaching me.

And I read Bert's poems. His capacity to visualize, to embody metaphor, stunned me. "I see it exactly!" I would think, encountering his images: two sailboats like tennis shoes walking on water; garlic whose "breath is a verb"—how entirely apt! As anyone who has tried to write a concrete and resonant image, or tried to teach someone else to write one, knows: it's hard. What's required? Devotion to both the five-sense fact of a thing and the dream it inspires; the facility to render it with the rhythmic and sonic pleasure that powers poetry; to compose it with the economic compression that is the signature of the poetic image; and to combine these craft elements into something that feels indelibly true to lived experience. Something like this:

> Smoke waters the flowers
> that grow in the lungs.
> The cigarette, like your life,
> is a piece of chalk
> that shrinks as it tries to explain.

A searing set of images from one of Bert's greatest poems, *After the Meal*, evoking the cancer that would kill him at 51.

* * *

Bert Meyers was a quintessential Los Angeles poet. Born there in 1928, his poems are full of evocations of "the desert that lost its mind": its freeways, vacant lots, gas stations, palm trees, dry hills, a place where "jasmine and gasoline / undress the night." The son of Romanian Jewish immigrants, he maintained lifelong ties to his Jewish heritage without being religious. In adulthood he worked as a janitor, a ditch digger, a sheet metal worker, a warehouse man, a printer's apprentice, and a house painter, until settling into work as an artisan picture framer and gilder, finding contract work with Los Angeles galleries. He once wrote in his journals, "I worked for more than fifteen years at various kinds of manual labor and during that time I met many men and women who could see and speak as poetically as those who are glorified by the printing press and the universities."

Self-taught, Bert dropped out of high school at sixteen only to find himself a college professor in the last years of his life. In between, he read everything. He had decided opinions about literature, especially canonical poets: "I think Yeats needs to be criticized," he wrote in his journals. "He, more than any other modern English poet, could make abstractions seem more real than our daily lives. Yet, his poems on women or old age are banal, for the way they portray sex as a kind of celestial gasoline and never deal with love." About Pound's Cantos he wrote: "I think the last stanza of 'Mary Had a Little Lamb' is of far more value to mankind."

If you've never read the whole of "Mary Had a Little Lamb," that last stanza has to do with kindness to the vulnerable. Bert was involved with various causes for his entire adult life, from working with communist youth in the 1940s and 50s to civil rights to the anti-Vietnam War movement. His poems often respond to the socio-political. It's uncanny to read a poem published in 1979 and feel its contemporary resonance: in "These Days" Bert writes, "These days, everything's bad. / The future waits in a button. / No one plans, nobody says: / Three years from now. . . ." The music and cultural critic Stanley Crouch said of Bert, "He was elegantly refined but also tough enough to understand the tragedy that slashes the throat of innocence."

Bert put a premium on honesty, writing to the poet John Haines: "The freedom to speak honestly to someone else is precious." He sent his second book, *The Dark Birds,* to W.H. Auden with a letter that closed: "I hope you enjoy the book. But if you dislike the poems, and have the time, I'd appreciate your telling me why." His fellow poet and friend Robert Mezey said of him, "Bert Meyers belonged to no school or coterie and had no use for fashion. He was that rarest of creatures, a pure lyric poet. His poems are very much what he was—gentle, cantankerous, reflective, passionate and wise."

* * *

Bert published five collections in his lifetime, all but one with small presses you've probably never heard of. His first book for instance, a chapbook called *Early Rain*, came out with the now-defunct Alan Swallow Press in 1960, when Bert was thirty-two. His most high-profile publication was *The Dark*

Birds, his second book and his first full length collection, which came out from Doubleday eight years later. It's in this book that Bert's mature style comes into full view, in poems like "Madman Songs" and "Stars Climb Girders of Light." For me and for many who are still alive and read Bert's work, many of his best known poems—"Signature," "After the Meal," "Some Definitions at Work," "Postcards," and "Pebble," to name but a few—can be found in this volume and in 1981's *The Wild Olive Tree & The Blue Café* (Jazz Press/PapaBach Editions), which came out a few years after his death. But to say "best known" in relation to Bert's work begs the question: best known by whom? He was read and respected by many of his contemporaries, including Robert Bly, Stanley Crouch, Denise Levertov, and Charles Simic. But he never published with a mainstream press like Doubleday again.

In 2007, nearly thirty years after he died, University of New Mexico Press brought out a collected, *In a Dybbuk's Raincoat*, which is how new and younger readers found his work. Small presses, university presses—Bert's work would not have survived without them. Considering the financial precarity such presses continually face, it's no surprise that all of Bert's books are out of print.

Which brings us to now. Nearly forty years after I first walked into the Bert Meyers Poetry Room, I've had the luck to edit this volume of his work. My co-editor, Adele Elise Williams, and Bert's son, Daniel Meyers, have been integral to this endeavor. I extend special gratitude to Daniel, who has kept his father's archive of poems, journals, letters, notes, and photos alive: this book would not exist without Daniel's stewardship of Bert's memory.

Readers will notice I keep referring to Bert as "Bert," and not "Meyers," which would be the convention for a book on a literary figure—I can't help it. As a student at Pitzer College, no one I met who had known Bert referred to him as anything else. There was often a sense of familial love, reverence, and bemusement in the way his former students and colleagues talked about him. Even though I never met Bert, I began to feel part of this family, part of the protective and loving circle that seemed to surround his memory and his work. In fealty to this, we've designed this book to move a bit like a circle, a necklace of poems studded here and there with someone's memory of Bert, someone's reading of his poetry, someone's photo of him, and other memorabilia. The poems are the central chain that link it all.

I want to thank Bert's former students—Amy Gerstler, Garrett Hongo, Ari Sherman, and Maurya Simon—as well as Bert's former colleagues at Pitzer College, Jim Bogen and Barry Sanders—for offering their memories of Bert to this volume. They bring his living presence to these pages. Thank you to Daniel Meyers for gifting us his indelible portrait of Bert as a father. Thank you to poets José Angel Araguz, Victoria Chang, and Sean Singer for bringing their reading minds to bear on three of Bert's poems, illuminating them for readers. Thank you to Adele Elise Williams for her enlightening look at Bert's work through the lens of gender studies. Thank you to Martin Rock for transforming all the raw material into a book. Thank you to the Nancy Luton Fund for invaluable support. Lastly, a deep bow to Kevin Prufer and everyone on the board of the Unsung Masters Series: this series makes space for the recovery and reclamation of significant literary voices nearly lost to time.

BEGINNINGS

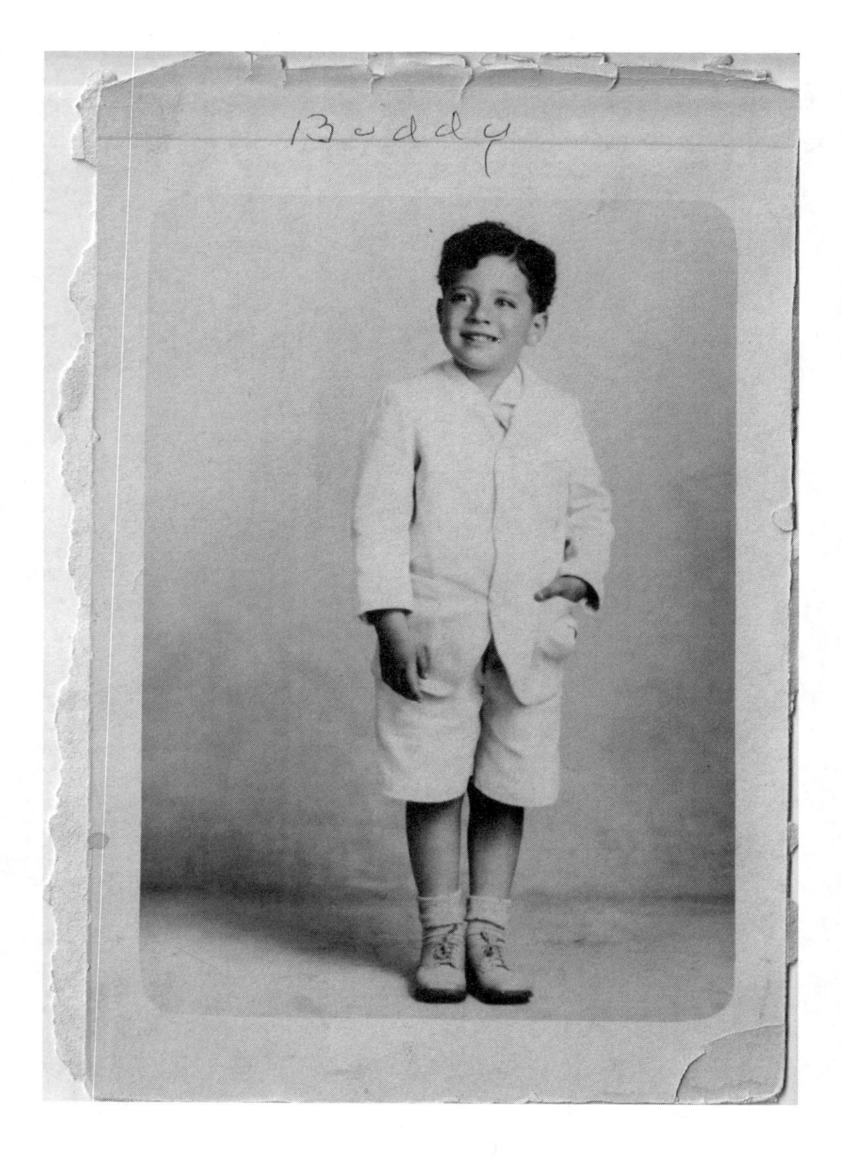

Bert, “Buddy,” about five years old, circa 1933.

CELLO: A MEMOIR

Garrett Hongo

In school at Pomona College in Southern California I took on extra courses my sophomore year to fulfill some requirements. I wanted the luxury the following term to study with Bert Meyers, a poet I'd heard about who taught at Pitzer College, an affiliated school in the same town. Other students I'd admired had studied with him, and they'd written poems that impressed me. I had to find out about this poet. I wanted to study with Bert Meyers.

I'd see him around the combined campuses. He was a Jew. The story was, Meyers himself had never gone to college but had been admitted to a graduate school in literature on the strength of his poetry. He'd been hired, then, without completing the Ph.D. He was a poet. His face was sharp like an axeblade's, his hair silvery and wiry and full of curls, ruffled like the surface of a lagoon just before a big rain. It rode up against one side of his head and seemed to crest there and hold itself like the high face of a large wave, poised just before crashing. He had eyes like a dromedary and smoked long brown unfiltered cigarettes that came in a red cardboard box. But it was his voice, a deep and resonant baritone rising to tenor, that summoned everyone when he spoke. It seemed to me that he did not actually speak, but was softly bowing, with the velvet cords in his throat, the strings of a tiny Cremona cello that was embedded there. His sentences came slowly, lavishly, with music and deliberation as if they were scored. At a public lecture, I heard him talk about "Baud'laire," and it seemed as if he were speaking of a beautiful, sickened forest, restored to life by energetic rains. He talked about Aimé Césaire of Martinique, about the Caribbean and the poetry of "Negritude," and his words sparked fresh thoughts through my mind concerning my own native land. A visiting poet from the Midwest, decked out in a varicolored Mexican poncho, once teased him about the largeness of his eyes, and Meyers said "Fuck you" out loud and flipped the arrogant visitor the bird. I decided this Meyers guy was for me. I took his class the next term.

It met in the evening, and I arrived a little late for the first session. The poet nodded to me to take the only seat available, which was next to him in the small seminar room. There were less than a dozen others in the class, all scruffy and long-haired, pseudo-hippie types of the middle to upper class.

I noticed Meyers had brought his own Thermos of coffee to class, a big blue-and-silver stainless-steel thing like the one my father carried to work on the night shift. The poet sipped while the little workshop of student poets talked.

A man with long blond hair and a puckered face that gathered down to a ginger beard introduced the topic of Walt Whitman and his homosexuality. A woman with long, braided brown hair, smelling of patchouli oil, cited some critics and a discussion about the same thing at a conference she'd attended in Vermont that past summer. I felt awe at how complicated their acquaintanceship with the subject was, how *socialized*. I'd barely begun to read poetry, let alone discuss it with adults in a public place.

Meyers said, "That's bullshit," then proceeded to provide us with an extended critique of this particular journalistic and decidedly unliterary approach to the discussion of Whitman. He said that Whitman was a poet who may have been gay, who may not have been gay, who might have been multi-sexual or bisexual or nonsexual, but what was important about him was that he had this feeling for humankind, for the wounded dying in the Union hospitals, for the *workers* and *builders* and *teamsters* and for *women* that compelled him to write a strange, prosaic, but chantlike non-metric verse, slightly imitative of what he thought *Indian* Vedic scripture was like, slightly imitative of what he thought Native American storytelling and ceremonial chant were like, and taking off on what he'd vaguely heard about as *vers libre* from the French; that Whitman had borrowed certain common American *religious* ideas; that he had joined all of these to what he felt was the elite fashion of literary Transcendentalism and, from that, he, Walt Whitman, a newspaperman and profound sentimentalist, had accomplished the building, along with Emily Dickinson, a spinster, of what had come to be our *American* poetry. Homosexuality was *not* the issue, nor was *heterosexuality*. It was *poetry* that was the issue and he,

Meyers, would not allow our discussions to be turned over to whatever fashionable or scholarly controversies had arisen to divert attention away from what was important. *Poetry was poetry*, he said, and although gay rights and women's rights and minority rights were important, it was *poetic content* and *poetic style* and *poetic tradition* which we would emphasize, and not the social controversies, not the debunking and not the dismissing. Unlike my usual literature professors who cultivated a studied mildness, Bert Meyers had passion, he had opinions, and he was not afraid to use them. He had an attitude, and he felt confident in exposing us to it. And that attitude had the music of eloquence.

There were some student poems handed out and read. Meyers said critiques would begin the following week. He ended the class session by reading aloud some translations from postwar Polish poetry—poems commemorating the work of rebuilding the country and its culture in the aftermath of World War II. He read from a pamphlet—an issue of a literary magazine. No books were yet available, he said. When he was finished, he tucked the pamphlet into his coat pocket, reassembled his coffee Thermos, and started for the door. He asked if I'd walk with him, as I'd said nothing during class, and it puzzled him.

We left the building through a glass door. His wife and teenage son and daughter were there to meet him. They were walking the family dog, a black Labrador, and invited me to trail along. We trudged back through a foggy night, across asphalt tennis courts, azalea-lined walks, and under olive trees. I found myself walking beside the poet, who'd produced a pipe and was having trouble keeping it lit. He'd stop from time to time, lighting the tobacco, and I'd stop with him to keep him company.

"I know why you're so pissed off," Meyers said, sucking on the stem of his pipe. Sprinklers hissed on a lawn somewhere nearby. His wife and children and dog were up ahead of us. I was stunned, fixed to the sidewalk in my sturdy tennis shoes. He stared at me.

"Your parents were in those Camps," he said, and a puff of smoke swirled around the dark blade of his face.

He said he'd been a kid in high school in Los Angeles. It was World War II, a few months after Pearl Harbor. He was a gymnast at Marshall High. There were lots of Japanese American kids in his school. He'd grown up with them. He'd gone to the picnics in MacArthur Park, where the Nisei would bring their kids every weekend and share food—rice balls and fish cakes and sweet pieces of marinated meat. He'd run around with them, playing baseball, stealing hubcaps, trying to get dates, when, all of a sudden, one morning, *all the Japanese American kids were gone!* Just gone. He couldn't believe it. Our government had taken all of them, rounded them up like cattle and marched them off into trains and shipped them away to God-knows-where, to Kingdom Come, to concentration camps in the desert. His schoolmates were stunned, but everyone seemed to accept it after a while. His father Manuel raged about it at home. It was a crummy deal.

Bert Meyers knew about it. He could tell me. He could look into my eyes and see into the history I was not myself ready to address, to live by. He knew part of my story, the part no one knew or seemed to want to know, and he said he would help me with it. He was telling me that. I followed him.

Greybird

They screamed, Get out!
and I've become a pile
of trash that mumbles
to itself on the sidewalk
while others go toward home.

In a little room
behind my forehead,
people are talking about me.
They're at a table
and they have yellow voices.
I'm a bell
they've buried in the snow.

Sometimes I feel
so vast, the stars
come out upon my skin.
And, each night I hope
to meet a stranger
who'll be a friend . . .

A man drags a woman to a car;
a drunken streetlight
dribbles in the gutter;
the same fool stares
at the broken glass
in a parking lot,
as if it were the starry sky.

1950

Wilshire Bus

These ladies concentrate
on how they look.
No one's too friendly;
this place is public.

Dressed up like a gift,
delivered by the bus.
Each woman feels
unique, mysterious . . .

but sad to be unwrapped
again, at home—
that cave where everything's
asleep, assumed, and known.

1952

It's a Pleasure to Be Sick

You feel that world outside the skin
rising, rising, like a mountain,
to keep you down?
The child in man knows what to do:
lie in bed and dream it through—
it's a pleasure to be sick.

That girl you love, loves another?
Don't feel guilty, go to mother.
She'll be glad to have you.
It's dark and dull, but soft in there,
with only birth and death to fear.
It's such a pleasure to be sick.

But what of those who do lie down
too long to laugh or call it fun,
and no one can arouse?
They see the whole world wearing black
and, color-blind, they answer back:
it's a pleasure to be sick.

Most men exult in what they've done,
wearing achievement like a sun
that pulls the world to them.
But those who refuse to work for love
(afraid they'll never earn enough)
have gray haired hearts and cry, *Unfair*!
and woo the world with their despair.
It's their pleasure to be sick.

1953

We Thank the Heart

It came from nowhere,
the impossible car.
Some of his thin hair
is stuck in the glass.

There's so much blood
the warm sun walks
like Christ upon it.
A needle's eye
in his tattered head
is losing his life's
essential thread;
the crowd kneels down.
A siren blows.
The man tries
to straighten out
his body, like
a suit of clothes.

We see the tailor
in his chest.

And we thank the heart,
and nothing else,
that patched his head,
that he smiles at us
and isn't dead.

1960

The Accident

There's so much blood
the warm sun walks
like Christ upon it.

A needle's eye
in his tattered head
is losing his life's thread.

The crowd kneels down.

We see the tailor
in his chest
work overtime.

A siren blows.
The man tries
to straighten out
his body, like
a suit of clothes.

1968

IN A LITTLE ROOM / BEHIND MY FOREHEAD: ON BERT'S BEGINNINGS

Dana Levin

One of the great gifts of 2007's *In a Dybbuk's Raincoat*—the now out-of-print collected poems of Bert Meyers, edited by his son Daniel and Morton Marcus—was its inclusion of unpublished poems, especially those Bert wrote as a young man. We've included three here that struck us as particularly impressive, for a high school drop-out in his early to mid-twenties. In them, you can find first inklings of feelings and human experiences that would drive Bert's poems his entire writing life: encounters with outsiders and the dispossessed—those bells "buried in the snow," as "Greybird" puts it, in a poem Bert wrote at twenty-two—and his tender hope for human connection to hold sway over the collective forces of estrangement. Sometimes that tenderness could turn to bitterness born out of Bert's clear vision of human nature and society's iniquities, as in "It's a Pleasure to Be Sick," a song written at twenty-five. And in all three of the early poems we've included here, one can see how empathic and attentive Bert was to the people around him. "Wilshire Bus," a poem Bert wrote at twenty-four, is surprisingly knowing about the constricted and conventionalized life of a woman in early 1950's America, where coming home after a lively day in the city might be a disappointment, home being "that cave where everything's / asleep, assumed, and known."

Bert was also, even in his twenties, fluent in the language of transformation, mostly working in simile to create arresting images. In "Greybird," "the same fool stares / at the broken glass / in a parking lot, / as if it were the starry sky." Each lady on the Wilshire Bus is "dressed up like a gift . . . sad to be unwrapped/again." Bert also had an ear for melodic syntax and sound, as in "It's a Pleasure to Be Sick." Indeed, in his early poems, music-making is often at the forefront. As he develops his art, he focuses more on the vivid images for which he is best known.

You can see this development in the revisions Bert makes to "We Thank the Heart," from 1960's *Early Rain*, which result in "The Accident," published eight years later in *The Dark Birds*. What did Bert change? Pace and scope, for one. "We Thank the Heart" reads as if it were a film, a flowing narrative relayed by witnesses who see the car, the collision, the victim, the crowd, and the resuscitation as if from across the street; "The Accident" reads more as a set of stills, the camera of the poem presenting the scene frame by frame. Even though Bert uses nearly the exact same phrasing in both poems, stanza breaks in "The Accident" isolate the pool of blood (stanza 1) and the victim's "tattered head" (stanza 2) into discrete close-ups: they're no longer just two of many details in the unfurling motion of the central stanza in "We Thank the Heart." Bert also does away with the opening stanza of "We Thank the Heart," letting the new title, "The Accident," give the context for the ensuing scene. Then he drops us immediately into the vivid image of a Christ-like sun walking on a pool of blood—a startling visual opening.

"We Thank the Heart" offers a long and elegant weave of slant and exact end-rhymes; in privileging a set of stills over melodic movement in "The Accident," Bert shifts the primary craft effect of the poem from music to image. Why does he do this? Did he ultimately feel like the musical beauty of "We Thank the Heart" obscured *seeing* something important? I admit, my primary reaction on first reading the end of that central stanza in "We Thank the Heart" was pleasure in the sonic resolve of that weave, once "clothes" rhymes with "blows." But by the end of "The Accident," my gaze is fixed on the image of the victim trying to "straighten out / his body, like / a suit of clothes." I think this is where Bert at forty, in *The Dark Birds*, wants us to look. "We Thank the Heart" ends on the relief of the witnesses that the victim has not died; in "The Accident," Bert cuts the feelings of the witnesses completely out of the poem, refusing to resolve the shock of watching a man get hit by a car. As Bert revises "We Thank the Heart" into "The Accident," harmonious rhyme yields to a haunting image, an image that could stand as an emblem for so much of Bert's work: a lone man trying to recover, after being struck.

Bert, gymnast. About age 17.

LOS ANGELES CITY HIGH SCHOOL DISTRICT

John Marshall High School

3939 TRACY STREET
LOS ANGELES 27, CALIFORNIA

W. BRUCE KIRKPATRICK
PRINCIPAL

VIERLING KERSEY
SUPERINTENDENT OF SCHOOLS

April 24, 1946

Mr. Manuel Meyers
3938 Tracy Street
Los Angeles 27, California

Dear Sir:

I trust that by now your son, Bertram, has seen fit to deliver the message which Mr. Boyd and I recently directed him to convey to you and that he has explained fully the predicament in which he has placed himself.

Our message which we first asked him to deliver was that we should like to have either you or Mrs. Meyers come to the school for a conference relative to his recent forcible entry into the gymnasium building and his subsequent refusal to give his name to the head custodian who was in charge of the building at that time. Your son returned to the office at the appointed time on the day following our original conference with him and stated that he would not deliver our message under any circumstances. Mr. Boyd and I not only endeavored to point out to him the seriousness of his entrance into the gymnasium, which as you know was at least the second time he has made illegal entry into the school buildings, but we also endeavored to convince him of his responsibility to acquaint you with his difficulties and urge you to come to the school. Bud steadfastly refused to comply with our request and became exceedingly arrogant and disagreeable in manner. We took occasion at that time to repeat to him the reports recently obtained from his teachers which indicate that his attitude is greatly in need of improvement and that he is failing at present in English, and was also failing in mathematics at the end of the first ten weeks. His teachers also commented upon his unsatisfactory attendance. Your son insinuated that the teachers were incorrect in their estimates of him and his work, and because of his most recent difficulty, as well as his unsatisfactory citizenship record for practically every semester of his attendance at John Marshall, and his disobedience in complying with our requests, I deemed it necessary to inform him that he has excluded himself from John Marshall High School.

In view of the fact that Bud is eighteen years of age he is not governed by the Compulsory Attendance Law and, therefore, there is no need for him to transfer to another school unless he desires to do so, in which case it would be necessary for him to find a school which would accept him under the circumstances. Also, in view of the fact that I had previously filed a letter requesting his deferral with his Selective Service Board,

Letter expelling Bert from John Marshall High School.
Bert would later become a college professor.

-2-

Mr. Manuel Meyers
April 24, 1946

I was required by law to notify the Board that his school record had become unsatisfactory both because of scholarship and citizenship and to withdraw my request for his deferral.

I sincerely regret that Bud has failed to respond properly to the many requests and suggestions made by Mr. Boyd and other members of the school and that the several conferences held between Mr. Boyd, Mrs. Meyers, and Bud seem to have been ineffective. I regret that a boy who was so close to graduation made it impossible for him to graduate both by reason of his academic failures and his unsatisfactory citizenship, and I sincerely trust that when and if Bud realizes his mistake he will see fit to continue his studies in such school as may be open to him. As yet your son has not officially cleared his record at John Marshall and I trust that you will urge him to return to the school from which he is now absent and surrender his books and any other equipment which he may have at the earliest possible moment.

Very truly yours,

W. Bruce Kirkpatrick
Principal

WBK.A

"Our message which we first asked him to deliver was that we should like to have either you or Mrs. Meyers come to the school for a conference relative to his recent forcible entry into the gymnasium building and his subsequent refusal to give his name to the school custodian . . . Bud steadfastly refused to comply with our request and became exceedingly arrogant and disagreeable in manner . . . Your son insinuated that the teachers were incorrect in their estimates of him and his work . . . "

Bert poses with a bicycle, 16 years old.

Bert in his early twenties.

I turned to poetry the way a man turns to a woman, ~~in~~
in order to live; the way an animal moans or a
birdsings, to relieve myself of pain and joy.

words, to me, are
~~I was nourished by words, those~~ sonorous nipples —
each one a lozenge full of memories under the tongue, a lig
in ~~the~~ throat.

I found Whitman and believed a poet should express
his country; Rilke and pitied my ~~bourgeois self~~ middle-class self for
a while; Blake and ~~discovered~~ saw politics in every line;
Issa and ~~worshipped his very compassion and humility~~ wished to be so compassionate + humble.

&

Emily Dickenson taught me to rely on metaphor; Yeats
~~gave me the courage to trust~~ showed me the value of music in a time of
portentous prose. Ten years as a picture framer and
gilder convinced me that even poems should be
beautifully made.

I've known waitresses and janitors from whom great
images flowed ~~like~~ as naturally as traffic on a freeway. I ~~enjoy~~ prefer
fairy tales ~~more than I do~~ to most literature and ~~was~~
I ~~know~~ believe that the last stanza of "Mary had a little Lamb"
is ~~f~~ more profound than The Cantos or ~~the~~ The Wasteland

Bert's notes on poetry.

THE WORK

A GARDENER IN PARADISE: A MEMOIR

Amy Gerstler

> *"And he still dreamed of a style*
> *so clear it could wash a face,*
> *or make a dry mouth sing."*

Reading Bert Meyers cleanses the senses. His poems intimately connect a reader to the physical gifts of the earth, to truly being an animal, and to the living, trembling moment. When I need to ground myself, touch the essential natures of things, I read Bert Meyers. As I read him, I have the illusion that I can somehow hold his images in my hands, like cherished toys. *Bread, insects, orchards, windows, rags, brooms, seeds, weeds, birds, children, ashes, a hammer and nails.* Even *the sun, moon, and stars.* His images are that tactile, concise, and alive.

When I want to remind myself of the power of small things, I read Bert's lines: "I like the subtle snail: / . . . and where it goes, it paints / the ground with useless roads." For me, this recalls Guy de Maupassant's quote, "The smallest thing has something unknown in it." Bert's poems teach us to gaze intently, with our whole, hungry souls, and to recognize immensities in the seemingly simple, the apparently humble, the easily overlooked.

Bert's poems make me think of Francis Ponge (in their fascination with objects and animals) and Marc Chagall (in their Jewish dreaminess) and eastern European poets like Charles Simic and Attila Jozsef. When I try to recall him as teacher (I briefly knew Bert! His work and his generosity as a writing professor changed my life!) I remember his famous cumulous whirl of curly, grey-white hair, which did look like smoke. I remember the slim, elegant cigarettes he puffed incessantly. (Were they Galouises?) These cigarettes (unfiltered?), which seemed to me synonymous with real literary sophistication, eventually killed Bert. I also remember the gap between his front teeth which lent his grin a roguish note.

The anger detonations in his poems are controlled but potent: I am emboldened and comforted by those ruptures. I love Bert's skepticism about so-called civilization and how he shakes his fist at it. Some of his poems compare civilization's effects on nature to that of an encroaching disease. Edward Germain, in the introduction to *English and American Surrealist Poetry* (an anthology that contains three of Bert's poems) wrote of the surrealist poets' ". . . need to create a vision superior to the ugliness of contemporary civilization." An apt observation about Bert's work. Did Bert consider himself a surrealist? I would have loved to have been able to ask him that.

Relatedly, Bert's poetry has, for all its lyricism, an anti-authoritarian strain. He rears up from time to time against soul-killing aspects of American life. That and his concern for the despoilment of the planet are among the qualities that make his work so timely. There is a feeling in some of the poems of a man who allows himself to see and feel everything, to revel in myriad forms of beauty and darkness, but who is also keeping himself in check, in order to live a humane and ethical life, albeit on his terms. And hovering inside the work too is a sense of incipient rebellion against those forces that repress him unreasonably, meanly, or too much. He sometimes chafes against an excess of social constraint, propriety, and domestication. Forces that hinder us all, in different ways.

When I read Bert's poem "Signature," containing the lovely phrase "a gardener in paradise," I became curious about whether Jewish notions of paradise include gardens. I found this sentence describing one model of Jewish paradise: "Each day in Paradise one wakes up a child and goes to bed an elder, thus enjoying the pleasures of childhood, youth, adulthood, and old age." Bert died at fifty-one, so he never got to enjoy the "pleasures of old age," whatever those might be. But the voice in his poems does seem to me the voice of someone ageless, or who is all ages at once, a wanderer who in each poem can speak from his child, youthful and adult selves seamlessly, and perhaps also from some far-seeing, archetype-rich, ancient, collective self. So, I wish you there, Bert, with all my heart, into that particular vision of Jewish paradise.

Signature

I earn a living
and I have a family
but to tell the truth
I'm a wild olive tree

I like cognac
and a proud Jewish song
I live wherever
I don't belong

I watch the world decay
on every page on every face
it's a sick man's clouded eye
that rolls around in space

And my obsession's
a line I can't revise
to be a gardener
in paradise

1979

And, Sometimes It Seems

And, sometimes it seems
that: because a man,
being born in a tear
when his mother wept,
never takes off his sweat
or really finds a friend,
already in the cradle
makes his little fist.

But what a brave thing
he is, who has a fountain
at his hips, a brain:
that blossom on the spine!

And, when I look at the earth
and the earth is someone
I love, then it seems:
what a pity man
becomes a melancholy
beast that likes to think.

1960

Rainy Day

Outside, nothing moves: only the rain
nailing the house up like a coffin.

Remember, in childhood, when it rained?
Then, the whole world sailed down the alley:

leaves, paper, old shoes, the buildings,
everything like a circus going to sea.

Now, the rain, the iron rain, with its little keys
is closing all the doors . . .

and I think we're all dead. See how the sky
sits like a tombstone on the roofs.

1960

The Garlic

Rabbi of condiments,
whose breath is a verb,
wearing a thin beard
and a white robe;
you who are pale and small
and shaped like a fist,
a synagogue,
bless our bitterness,
transcend the kitchen
to sweeten death—
our wax in the flame
and our seed in the bread.

Now, my parents pray,
my grandfather sits,
my uncles fill
my mouth with ashes.

1960

At Night

At night, when the mouse
is murdered by cheese,
when the tired walls turn away,
when the body can't stand anymore,
then death parts my hair
and I don't want to die.
I don't want to die!

The asthma weeps.
The asthma burns in its leaves.
The medicines consult,
aware of their labels,
by the bed.

But death comes:
out of the faucets, the floors,
from the big clock that bleeds
weakening in its springs,
it comes shoveling out my chest.
And I don't know why
but I know the heart beats
and beats a man to death.

1960

Origin

Daily the sea sprayed my town
with gulls . . . it could have murdered me.
I took a shell whose mask of tides
was a refinement of the sea.

The brawny boats went where they pleased;
I traveled in a twisted bone.
That's how I discovered islands
where hungry shadows quarry stone.

1960

In Those Mountains

In those mountains, time filled
one bush with castor beans,
another with wild roses . . .
Death was something distant
that made a buzzard stir
its whirlpool in the sky.

By a tree, I found the deer
hunters lost—a flower
of ants in the bullet hole
and a root held its leap.

There sunlight came down
a trail and green nature
reddened at the tip.
Yucca struck at the wind,
turned dull and rusted
in the fall. Lizards
split the rocks, then ran;
snakes passed and left their clothes.

Below, a little town,
like a tumor, began to spread.

1960

At My Window

Across the street
nine boys in the weeds scream,
hurling rocks. Blackbirds
are headlines overhead.

One boy looks at the sun.
And I look back at how
I stood, under a tree,
my hands hot with stones.
A squirrel, tail up
and balanced on a bough,
faced me like a question
I couldn't answer.

Here, on this jewel of earth,
time tears at the green edge.
This pane, thin water,
makes two small islands
of my eyes;
and the sky
always seems to be
the sail of a great ship
that never reaches land.

Below, on the sidewalk,
a neighbor's little girl,
tall as a yardstick,

her eyes in glasses,
on her bike rides by
singing, *Oh lady of Spain,*
I adore you . . .

1960

When She Sleeps

When she sleeps I rise.
The naked light bulb burns
and makes the moths outside
beat against the screen.
A moth comes out of me.
It flies to the light,
then staggers back in pain
to rest in me again.
She sleeps and holds her peace,
though I'm consumed by this.

1968

STRANGING AND RETURNING: ON *WHEN SHE SLEEPS*

José Angel Araguz, Ph.D.

Prompted by a friend, I read Bert Meyers' *In a Dybbuk's Raincoat* several times, checked it out from the library as long as was allowed, and pored over his words. In them I found a sensibility so attuned to image and metaphor as to evoke another world beyond the page. Which is the goal of poems: to strange things up and return them to us so that all involved are changed.

This stranging and returning is found in "When She Sleeps." In it, the speaker sits awake while his partner has gone to bed; while sitting, he watches a moth "come out" of him, fly to the light, then "[stagger] back in pain / to rest in [him] again." The poem ends with the speaker remaining awake "consumed by this."

Note how the poem moves in parallels. There's the stagger of the moth away from the light that causes pain, a parallel to the stagger of the sleepless speaker. There's also the parallel of being consumed—the moth literally, the speaker figuratively.

Note, too, how "moth words" and "human words" are juxtaposed, blurred through associations. The stagger of one becomes that of the other, as noted above, and the pain of one transfers to the other as well. This aptness for images infused with emotional resonance is a mark of Meyers. He schools you without needing footnotes. Deceptively spare at times, Meyers works a poetic line whose engaging difficulty is born not of linguistic denseness nor erudition but from a clarity that demands attention.

This difficulty is apparent when one considers how the poem ends on the word "this," a fruitful ambiguity which allows the reader room to take "this" literally (the speaker is consumed by the scene) or figuratively (the speaker is consumed by writing itself, by the world that poetry has laid not just before him but the reader as well). In this manner, Meyers is one of those writers who trusts his readers to follow, to cotton to the moment, the image, the sense of revelation ready to unfold.

* * *

It matters too how my life had unfolded in the few years before I came across this Meyers poem, as this informs how moved I was by it. Shortly before, I had earned an MFA from New York University and moved across the country to Oregon, all while deep into what would end up being my first marriage. It was a tumultuous couple of years: I had just finished being in classes with writers who seemed more impressed with themselves than with poems. Some scoffed at being assigned the writing of sonnets. One was fond of reminding the workshop about his being on staff at *The Paris Review.* As for the writer who was a year ahead of me and who described my cohort—one comprised of writers primarily from marginalized backgrounds—as making the program "look different"—well, that was something else.

After two years of being in those rooms, my mantra, the words that I would mutter to myself storming out of workshops or simply walking dead tired through the city, became: *It's not my poetry that matters, it's poetry that matters.*

In Oregon, I was doing what I did during the MFA to survive: working jobs that had me up before dawn. Leaving my partner asleep, I'd stagger to the kitchen table and work out in poems whatever my mind could muster. Coming across "When She Sleeps" was like coming across a mirror. Like the speaker, I was awake while another slept. Like him, I staggered in my own flavor of pain.

Then and now, reading Meyers I feel as though I am being asked to take myself seriously as a human being. In a way, allowing a poem to teach you how it wants to be read is a practice that teaches humility on and off the page. Here, again, I think of the difficulty I noted earlier, how Meyers' work asks us not to stand in awe of the poem but of what the experience of the poem evokes. It's an act of attention and presence. That's the only way into his poems. At a time in my life when difficulty was a pervasive theme, and I didn't care to be present in my personal and professional spaces, I was creatively shocked awake by what this difficulty gave me: the light as well as the stagger. Perhaps it's better to say that his work invites readers to reckon with, as well as revel in, their humanity.

As moths keep coming in and out of my poems, talking to me, solving mysteries, soothing the face of the moon, I remain consumed by what is possible in all of *this*.

They Who Waste Me

When I ask for a hand,
they give me a shovel.
If I complain, they say,
Worms are needles at work
to clothe a corpse for spring.
I sigh. Whoever breathes
has inhaled a neighbor.

1968

Gulls Have Come Again

Gulls have come again
to consider another beautiful death of the sun.

People were flowers that grew by the shore;
twilight takes them home,
they fade together at their tables.

In the tall green shops the pulleys of birds
lower the last light,
the eyelid of a shadow shuts the hills,
the sound of the ocean walks over the land.

Nobody wants to die.

1968

Funeral

Surely a dead moth's
the skull of a tiny horse,
and the moon's a saint
who pities the sea.

Peace, peace to this child
of rain and light,
and the people who stay
holding candles and lilies,

tasting their tears,
naked in a dream,
over the long drawer
they've closed in the earth.

1968

Lullaby

1962, Cuban missile crisis

Go to sleep my daughter
go to sleep my son
once this world was water
without anyone

1968

A Year in a Small Town

1.

Surrounded by flowers,
bees are drowning
in the housepainter's pot.

2.

Today, I know
I haven't done as much
for this world as a tree.

3.

Children bring home
stones instead of friends;
the blackbird has a golden eye.

4.

Spring, that young man
is wearing the shirt
I was wounded in.

1968

Pigeons

Wherever I go to find
peace or an island
under palms in the afternoon
at midnight to pity my neighborhood
at dawn in the shrubs
to look for a child

I hear them
they fly by
applauding themselves
I see them
they pray as they walk
their eyes are halos
around a pit
they look amazed

Who are these that come
as a cloud to our windows
who rush up like smoke
before the town burns

You will find one
on a mountain
in a carpenter's shop
at home on the lawn
of an old estate
at the library
in the forehead of paradise

Whoever is mad
can accuse them
thousands were killed in a day

What happens to them
happens to me
when I can't sleep
they moan and I'm there
and it's still like that

1968

The Dark Birds

The dark birds came,
I didn't know their name.

They walked in Hebrew on the sand
so I'd understand.

They sang, the sea flowed,
though no one made a road.

I shivered on the shore
when the water closed its door.

Then as I felt the birds return
to me like ashes to an urn,

and sunlight warmed the stones,
fire undressed my bones.

1968

BERT MEYERS, A JEWISH WRITER: ON *THE DARK BIRDS*

Sean Singer

I best understand Bert Meyers as a Jewish writer. Meyers' poems are Jewish poems: they're assimilated, but invisible; indebted to the Psalms and Proverbs, but seeking new texts. Being born into something as old as three millennia, but tasked with questioning everything about language, Meyers' poems are about knowing that since the Shoah, every word is broken and incomplete.

The voice in his poems exists on the periphery, and that voice is able to be the polestar and give meaning to the fable and the decay of experience.

Meyers' poems exist in a space of invisible difference, part of an unseen community, but moving in and out of fixed definitions. Existing as a poet, feeling that outsiderness in your body, having to go so deep into yourself, to envelope it and implicate it, is to be in an in-between place, an exile, holding a hatchet to cut new trails in the cartography. Jewish identity is like that, and his poems express it in the most chiseled and precise ways possible.

In "The Dark Birds" the rhymed couplets are intimate and vulnerable, and that either banishes dreams or inculcates pure ones. The birds have knowledge about the speaker of which even he is unaware: "They walked in Hebrew on the sand / so I'd understand."

The images of closure and impermanence ("didn't know," "sand," "no one," "closed," "like ashes," "undressed") are ways of showing the speaker's exclusion even as he has a communion with the birds, sand, sea, and sunlight pulsing around him. The turn in line ten, which is not end-stopped, implies the birds' return, and therefore their shared language also returns the speaker's core nature; his bones are undressed by the heat and light of the sun. This act of recovery is something accessible and also at a remove from experience.

The philosopher Emil Fackenheim said that the Nazi Genocide of the Jews was not for territory, money, or power; it was annihilation for the sake of annihilation. The problem of Auschwitz is also a problem of language: how can I be faithful to something even if there is no promise in it? A poem is what Vassily Grossman in *Life and Fate* called a "small goodness" from one person to another. This "small goodness" exists before it becomes a doctrine, policy, theology, organization, or institution, when it becomes deformed and abused. Meyers can be a voice of self-preservation, a will to be through language, a chance to understand the Other. When poets hammer out their own metaphors, they are also being reborn, attaching new meanings to dead symbols.

When poetry occurs at the margins, when we feel simultaneously seen and invisible, and when we are solitary from the dominant society, we are what Maxine Kumin called "secret Jews." For Jewish poets like me, like Meyers, this is doubly true. Jews are doubly in exile, doubly peripheral for having invented monotheism, psychoanalysis, and Marxism, and performing as being part of the world all the while being outside of it, *observing* and observing.

The Poet

1.

They said, Go, rise each day
with her, become
the reliable dough a family needs.
I wouldn't. I walked away
from the kitchen, the store
she was building in her breast . . .
And everything grows dim
like the little stone
brought home from the shore.

2.

What will I bring
if I come to your house?
A cold wind at the door,
bad dreams to your spouse.

There isn't a tree
in your backyard;
the lawns are plastic,
the chairs are too hard.

No, I wouldn't talk.
I'd be full of spite
and I'd strike my head
like a match that won't light.

3.

Woman, mirror of all my sides,
I pass through you to the window.

When I lay my hand on the grass
forgive me if I call the earth my child.

4.

Always poor, he knows
the crickets will leave him
small jars of money.

He waits, he admires a weed.
His dreams are addressed.

At night by his desk
he becomes a flower;
children are bees in his arms,
a little pain making honey.

1968

The Family

The boy will grow and be a man.
He'll have no father then.

The girl, assuming womanhood,
will burn herself in bed.

The father leaves the house at dawn.
The mother turns her dream-world on.

Still, night brings them all together,
to shriek and shudder.

1968

A Child's an Apple

Those who are tall look down.
They show their keys,
the dead birds in their hands.
They open and close
volumes of doors.
They smile.
Their teeth are the stones
in the graveyard at noon.
They're always hungry
and when they love they bite.

1968

Cigarette

Often you light a fuse
to prove you won't explode.
All the smoke shows
the power that dies in you.

You sigh as you tap
your way to the end.
The hand is the blind child
called to the blackboard.

1968

Madman Songs

1.

People go home
to rest in vaults
curtains soothe their faults
bright windows show their money
I hated home
it caused me pain
cloudy days
and evenings came
I leaned against
the iron rain

2.

Someone held me there was harm
now each word's an alarm
the man who looks so calm
will turn into a bomb
Woman daughter son
I wake up and put them on
they hide me from the law
My desire's a blade of grass
I trample as I pass
Fear me what I hate will fall

3.

In summer small cones
of dirt beside a fence
erupt with the weddings

of the ants
A moth staggers from a shrub
People turn their sprinklers on
to watch the water girls
dance on their lawn
I don't go out
until they've all gone in
They might come near
with large damp wings
love and other things

4.

When I don't sleep
the crickets weep

When I say
My life will pass
they scrape the dark glass

When the wall
begins to fall
where I strain
they file the chain

When I rise
I wear an orange shirt
A green woman
is rinsing her skirt
She imagines me

5.

David's gone Goliath's strong
flocks of pebbles bleat
their brittle cries of light
fade where the leaves lie
dry harps near a stream

Jacob warmed a rock
the rock and Jacob dreamed
I'm burning I'm alone
everyone's a stone
I break my feelings on

6.

I sat on the sidewalk
with my own box of chalk
and all day long I made
the whole world by myself
That's not the world they said

Then I rose at dawn
I put a label on
it wore me out by noon
All day I swung a brush
to see the buildings bloom

Just painting on a wall
won't change a man at all

or make the stone turn blue
So I sat down once more
What else could I do

7.

People go home
Twilight's a glass
through which they pass
The carver calms
his arm and leaves
his passion in the grain
The one who ran
runs back again
We live in pain
The moon's an aspirin

1968

Spleen

Sometimes, I just hang around
like a dead man's coat,
or a vacant lot that trembles
when construction crews pass.

I go to a coffee shop
and sit for hours to watch
a window's silent film—
people, scrawled and erased
on a long, gray page.

Later, when clouds blaze,
then suddenly grow old
and sad, I take a walk.

Evening begins with headlights
and a sound track of birds
that fades from tree to tree.
Behind a garage, a few
strange weeds, taller than men . . .

1979

BORN IN A TEAR: ON BERT MEYERS, GENDER, AND ADMISSION

Adele Elise Williams

When I first encountered Bert Meyers' poetry, after years in graduate school studying poetry and poetics, I realized two things: one, the number of tremendous unknown poets; two, poetry gatekeeping is real. Meyers should be taught widely and with regularity. Why was I reading William Carlos Williams, those *chickens*, that *wheelbarrow*, pining for *plums* (I don't even like plums!), when Meyers was saying things like, "Surely a dead moth's / the skull of a tiny horse, / and the moon's a saint / who pities the sea" ("The Funeral"). Like many readers, I was first wooed by Meyers' imagery and condensed lyric, but I was also immediately struck by his engagement with gender.

Take for example "And, Sometimes it Seems," from Meyers' first book *Early Rain*. Meyers frames the poem within a gendered dichotomy; it is the poem's essential instigation. The first full line reads, "And, sometimes it seems / that: because a man, / being born in a tear / when his mother wept, / never takes off his sweat / or really finds a friend, / already in the cradle / makes his little fist." In much of Meyers' poetry men are fated, faulty, and burdensome while women are everything possible, are superior in their life-giving and their optimistic duration—"Woman, mirror of all my sides" ("The Poet"). Significantly, this distinction never feels yucky or cringy. At the risk of cliche, it is clear to me that Meyers writes from his heart. This is especially apparent in poems about his family. In "Gently, Gently," after evoking the challenges the family has faced, he ends with this vow to his wife: "I swear by the wings / love spreads at my waist, / that I'll carry your tune / until my tired strings break." Additionally, Meyers writes about his own complicity; he still outs himself as a "dude," an outing that is particularly clear in "Madman Songs"— "Woman daughter son / I wake up and put them on / they hid me from the law / My desire's a blade of grass / I trample as I pass / Fear me what I hate will fall" and "I'm burning I'm alone / everyone's a stone / I break my feelings on." Meyers' acknowledgement of his own gendered faults is critical to his critique. His is not a redemptory poetics; Meyers does not tell us that he knows better, but rather that he simply *knows*. And he does not claim to be better for that knowing.

Was critiquing masculinity an intentional part of Meyers' poetics? I cannot be sure, but my instinct says no: it would be a rare thing to encounter poetry composed by a man in the nineteen seventies to make such critique; and this is why Meyers' positioning of men (and women for that matter) in his poetry is particularly provocative. When Meyers falls short, as he does as a citizen in "A Citizen" or father in "The Poet" for example, more often than not he understands his failings are inherent to his gender performance. I cannot help but find this incredibly prescient. His gendered self-analysis reveals much about the type of hu/man Meyers was—self-taught, a laborer, an under-recognized poet, a minority, *a melancholy beast that likes to think* . . . .

It is important how Meyers positions gender in his poetry, despite operating within received binaries, because it illustrates Meyers' perceived failings as a man: "I am a coat hanger / twisted by rage. / Everything shrinks from my hands— / that landscape threatened by planes, / a woman's astonished face" ("A Citizen"); Meyers' lyrical critique of masculinity is impactful because he is critiquing himself. One might glean from his poetry, as I am doing now, that Meyers felt inadequate in this masculinity: Meyers was the child of immigrants; he was a high school dropout and of the working-class; he was a self-taught poet and less recognized than his peers. Though he may have fallen victim to typical (and taught) expectations of male performance, Meyers resented aspects of it while also, naturally, hoping for success and achievement in the roles of father, teacher, and poet. These conflicting positions, critiquing a masculinity that one feels inferior to in the first place, doesn't just reveal much about Meyers, it illuminates the complexity, the nuance, of being a desirous person at all.

As a poem pondering a flawed male existence, "Spleen," from *The Wild Olive Tree*, can be read as a response to the final lines of "And, Sometimes it Seems"— "what a pity man / becomes a melancholy / beast that likes to think"— as "Spleen's" lyric is wholly interior. Meyers hangs around "like a dead man's coat," moving slowly through an urban space, observing (*thinking*) with a mood of defeat and gloom. He trolls a "vacant lot that trembles" and then watches the silent film of a coffee shop's commerce—"people, scrawled and erased / on a long, gray page." The clouds "grow old and sad." Then the poem ends "Behind a garage, a few / strange weeds, taller than men. . . ." It is the quiet resignation of this line that gets me. Meyers' poems are rarely loud and dramatic, and in this way they feel all the more personal. Meyers is not performing; he observes strange weeds taller than himself and recognizes that even nature, lacking ego and insecurity, still out-thrives him.

I wish I had read Meyers before (how can I have just learned of him!), though it feels especially important to read Meyers now. As a true autodidact, Meyers champions the underdog. His poetry often concerns the silenced, the striving, those on the margins, yet critically, Meyers does not applaud himself for doing this work. Rather, he admits his own shortcomings: "the man who looks so calm / will turn into a bomb" ("Madman Songs"). These admissions of falling short as a man are what I find so very profound— they do not instruct, they do not offer solutions, they do not claim to be more than disclosure. And they are particularly spiritual—as a Jew Meyers was no stranger to atonement. Though Meyers leans into his own darkness, his own gendered faults, there is still reverence in these poems. There is light, and so I would like to end there. As any spiritual body or rooted plant knows, it is only from darkness that there can be sun, and so, with his big bleeding heart, Meyers shows us some sun too: "I feel like a streetlight / tall and radiant / my face was made to shine among the others."

FREE LUNCH: A MEMOIR

Jim Bogen

Some time after Bert was appointed to the Pitzer College faculty, he asked to be given free lunches in its dining hall. Granting his request accomplished several things of value to Bert. The first was free meals. The economic values of even the smallest transactions concerned him greatly. In addition to this, the free lunches gave him a chance to hang out and talk—usually about culture and politics—in an informal, out of the classroom setting. Sometimes he told us about writers and literature we should know about. Bert was largely self-taught. He learned a lot by reading in public libraries, including the one in a juvenile hall where he spent a fair amount of time in his youth as a truant and a juvenile delinquent. Most auto-didacts don't have such good teachers.

And he felt as strongly about literature as true believers feel about their religions. In many memorable Passovers he replaced the most religious parts of the Haggadah with readings from Jewish literature. I remember him beginning these portions with 'If I were a Rothschild,' from a famous bit by Yiddish actor and writer Sholem Aleichem.

During one Pitzer lunch he answered questions about metaphor and said that almost anything could be a metaphor for almost anything else. I asked him for an example: how could a tree be an ice cream cone? He answered immediately: On an autumn afternoon the wind is blowing leaves off a tree. The wind is a licking tongue. The tree is the ice cream cone it's licking.

Here is one of my favorites among Bert's images. A worker is going home at the end of a hard day. Describing the sky above him, Bert says, "We live in pain / The moon's an aspirin." Images like this were his main gift to readers.

"Bert had been a gymnast in his youth and apparently loved to walk around on his hands to amuse his friends."—Maurya Simon.

Bert in 1977. "I worked for more than fifteen years at various kinds of manual labor, and during that time I met many men and women who could see and speak as poetically as those who are glorified by the printing press and the universities."—Bert's journals.

No more poems for awhile.
I've joined the Gilder's Maffia:
every night we take our tips
to battle the clan of Munn
and clothe the married limbs
of wood with gold.

The agate's mightier than the pen.

Bert
March 20, 1960

Bert writing in his journals, 1960.

"Prior to his tenure at Pitzer College, Bert's jobs included serving as a janitor, farm laborer, printer's apprentice, and house painter. Later he became an artisan picture framer and gilder. The skills and craftsmanship required in these pursuits engendered Bert's deep respect for the worker's tools, which carries over into his poems."—Maurya Simon. *Photo by Seymour Linden, 1967.*

Stars Climb Girders of Light

Stars climb girders of light.
They arrange themselves
in the usual place,
they quit before dawn,
and nothing's been done.

Then men come out.
Their helmets fill the sky;
their cities rise and fall
and men descend,
proud carpenters of dew.

Man brief as the storm,
more than five feet of lightning,
twisted and beautiful.
Man made like his roads,
with somewhere to go.

1968

Picture Framing

My fingers graze in the fields of wood.

I sand pine, walnut, bass,
and sweat to raise their grain.

Paints, powder and brush,
are the seasons of my trade.

At the end of the day
I drive home
the proud cattle of my hands.

1968

Twilight at the Shop

A whole day at the saw—
when they come for the rubbish,
I throw myself
out with the dust.

We smile and smoke and praise
what's left of the sun.
Dark trees have bottled its light.
They glow like many beers.

1976

Some Definitions at Work

The hammer lowered its horns
and the rusty nail shrieked
pulled from the place where it lived

The table-saw whined
like a virtuous bee
that knows it will die
in a meadow of dust

The sandpaper sighed
as it killed itself
caressing the sugar pine the ash

The housepainter's brush
hermaphrodite
with a long stem a vaginal voice
and a spring in its bristle
swayed satisfied with itself on the wall

Glue the woodworker's sperm
began to boil in the pot

The rags their breath
full of turpentine
demanded their rights
and threatened to burst like the sun

Then the woman
who turned into a mop
disheveled gray
worn out by the floor

and the man
who'd become a broom
his broad shoulder
lost in the dirt

noticed how even a motor
bleeds when it breaks
drops of oil stare from its skin
like the eyes of frightened fish

1979

Pencil Sharpener

It has no arms or legs, this tiny nude; yet grip it by the waist, then stir its hips: a dry leaf multiplies, a cold motor starts in the wood.

Revived, still shivering, the pencil sheds itself—and there's a butterfly, teeth, the fragments of a crown.

1979

The Old Engraver

An old engraver was out of work. He lived alone with his tools. It was summer. The sky wore jeans and every day the backyard opened its familiar shop: a worm scrolling along, the trees elaborating themselves.

But in the street children were grinding each other between the gears of their parents' wrath. Should he just walk around without a point?

So, each morning he printed lots of money; and all the children went to the candy store and became sweet.

Then, the police appeared. The old engraver was out in the yard, hanging dollars up to dry with his underwear.

He had to go to jail. And all the children turned into broken glass until even the mountains, those solitary herds, bled to death.

The moon, a giant freezer, hummed. It was going to be used.

1979

The Gilder

The Shop, weakened by dust, was closing its eyes. The saw stopped like an ambulance. A breeze made of turpentine still hung around his hands.

Outside, the walls in the alley were gold leaf fluttering on their frames; clouds, retired housepainters, relaxed in the sky.

A little cello began to throb in his throat.

Suddenly, he saw the sun overturn like a truckload of oranges at the end of a street—its light scatter and roll through the windows on a hill.

What's that got to do with Wittgenstein, or how we live? voices shouted in his head.

Nothing . . . nothing at all.

1979

Landscapes

1. The City

The city grows
from a highway's stem:
it's a glittering circuit board,
a crystal that palpitates.

Night's swept away
like a broken glass.

The day begins.
It prints the parking lots;
doors work like switches;
people are impulses in a system.

But often, a siren occurs—
the awakened man's incredulous wail.

And the sky, that rotten lung,
bleeds, then blackens;
the windows on the walls
multiply their cells

Still curious, the infected moon
regulates its lens.

2. On the Outskirts

On the outskirts, the factory—
somebody's chemistry set;
a junkyard, where the town
keeps throwing itself away;
rust clots on the mangled iron;
pain in the sun's aluminum glare . . .

There's a hubcap, going blind
in a ditch; the dust,
spreading its cataract;
and a few yellow machines
that die like sunflowers,
dropping their parts in a field.

The hills are a pile of rags
in a pail of dirty thinner;
scrap metal trees crinkle
in the wind's gray flame;
and the tumbleweeds roll
their barbed wire over the roads . . .

An airplane roars like a sperm
through a crack in the smog's deep stone.

3. Along the Coast

You stare (propped like a sick man)
from the car's enchanted bed.

A hill nibbles at a field's green fork;
an old arthritic fence
hobbles up toward a cloud.

A little factory smoke
grows abstract in the sky.

Only the cows have reached perfection.
Their quiet minds look empty.
The landscape requires them . . .
When the cows eat, the ground,
the shadows, even boulders,
rise and bow to each other.

Far away, the suburbs—
one cube cloning itself, like the stone
at the veterans' cemetery.

And all along the coast
the sun drives over the sea.
Its windshields glitter in the waves.

1979

L. A.

The world's largest ashtray,
the latest in concrete,
capital of the absurd;
one huge studio
where people drive
from set to set and everyone's
from a different planet.

For miles, the palm trees,
exotic janitors,
sweep out the sky at dusk.
The gray air molds.
Geraniums heat the alleys.
Jasmine and gasoline
undress the night.

This is the desert
that lost its mind,
the place that boredom built.
Freeways, condominiums, malls,
where cartons of trash and diamonds
and ideologies
are opened, used, dumped near the sea.

1976

After the Meal

1.

A suburb of coffee cups;
napkins, those crumpled hills;
silverware, freeways
spotted with grease, with flesh . . .

and the ash-tray,
a ghetto full of charred men
with grizzled heads
who wasted their flame;
where every breath
scatters its bones
and small gray mounds
accumulate, then crumble,
like nations
or the knees of elephants.

2.

Like a cleaning plant, steam
comes through a hole in your face.
Your exhaust is the last
wild horse that gallops away.

3.

Smoke waters the flowers
that grow in the lungs.
The cigarette, like your life,
is a piece of chalk
that shrinks as it tries to explain.

1979

To My Enemies

I'm still here, in a skin
thinner than a dybbuk's raincoat;
strange as the birds who scrounge,
those stubborn pumps
that bring up nothing . . .

Maddened by you
for whom the cash register,
with its clerical bells,
is a national church;
you, whose instant smile
cracks the earth at my feet . . .

May your wife go to paradise
with the garbage man,
your prick hang like a shoelace,
your balls become raisins,
hair grow on the whites of your eyes
and your eyelashes turn
into lawn mowers
that cut from nine to five . . .

Man is a skin disease
that covers the earth.
The stars are antibodies
approaching, your president
is a tsetse-fly . . .

1979

BERT MEYERS, A POLITICAL POET: ON *TO MY ENEMIES*

Victoria Chang

I'm drawn to Bert Meyers' poem, "To My Enemies," because of its spiky title. Meyers' title indicates a multitude of enemies, and it made me wonder: who are these enemies the speaker is referring to, and also what could the speaker say to them via this poem? The title also made me think about my own enemies and what I might say to them. In the literary world, it seems like it's more common to have enemies, multiple ones, than not to have any. In fact, in the age of rampant oversharing and social media, anyone is anyone's enemy, even for a second, since we are all being judged and judging all the time. Loyalties and alliances can change with the wind. The provocative title inspired all of these thoughts before I even started reading the poem!

Interestingly, the title sets up expectations, and yet the first stanza subverts those expectations by turning the mirror away from the enemies toward the speaker. The poem opens with a self-admission of the speaker's own inadequacies, a strategy that disarms the poem and shifts it from the accusatory to a more complex poem. This focus on the speaker maintained my attention while withholding the answer posed in the title—yet I was still wondering how Meyers could interest me in the speaker's enemies. This is the trouble of all poems, arguably: how to make the reader care about the speaker's concerns.

One way that Meyers makes a reader care is with his deployment of humor. Line breaks in the first stanza, and throughout the poem, play an important role in how the poem generates surprise. The first line breaks at "skin," making the reader think of regular human skin, but the next line adds the surprise of "a dybbuk's raincoat." Meyers often creates an additive effect that can lead to comic absurdity. The speaker's skin isn't just likened to a dybbuk's raincoat, but it's "thinner" than a dybbuk's raincoat. In a Meyers poem, it's as if everything has an extension cord, even the joke.

In the third stanza, the line break at "paradise" carries a double meaning, because the joke is that the speaker wishes the enemy's wife to go to paradise *with the garbage man.* The poem doesn't apologize for its tone of spite, something surely most of us have felt toward our own enemies! Rather, it seems to bask in its invective quality, and the ribbing is accepted because the speaker mocks himself in the first stanza and uses jokes to disarm the reader in the second.

The additive piling on of humor continues in the third stanza with the "prick" that hangs like a "shoelace" and the "balls" that become "raisins." These images are so simplistic and ludicrous that they have a comic absurdity to them, sounding like things a second grader might say to another second grader on the school yard. These takedowns feel authentic *because* of their impetuous, immature tone (and who hasn't had such absurd thoughts toward our own enemies)?

But then, the poem shifts in the next line to a creepy, surreal image of the hair growing on the whites of eyes. This shift reminds the reader that we are reading a real poem by a real poet, and not a second grader; after all, humans are complex—we can behave like second graders *and* be sophisticated poets. There's gravity in this shift and the feelings of the speaker gain seriousness. Here too, we see how Meyers' approach toward imagery is additive, extension-like. He keeps piling on the imagery, long after other poets might have stopped for fear of excess.

In the final stanza, Meyers expands the poem to something weightier than the second graders on the school yard: to "Man" at large. Imagine if the poem had begun with "Man"—we'd likely find the poem less powerful because of its obviousness and lack of nuance. Instead, Meyers draws the reader in, and we are ready for his telescopic argument. The poem reveals itself as a deftly rendered political poem.

The poem ends with "your president" in the penultimate line, implying a difference between the "your" and "my." The general "president" also clumps all presidents together, whether they are presidents of different countries, throughout time within a country, presidents of companies, or of the PTA. The ending of Meyers' poem is humorous and biting at once, like a tsetse fly. And suddenly we're back tonally to the second-grade schoolyard, but there's a seriousness to the assertion now, one that wasn't present in the prior stanza—we're nodding now, ruminating about the dangers of humans and how presidents are tsetse flies, and perhaps so are all of us.

"An autodidact who didn't finish high school, Bert Meyers was eventually admitted to Claremont Graduate School, based solely on the merit of his poetry. There he earned a master's degree in English, but, disillusioned by academia, he left before completing his PhD." —Maurya Simon.

A college for women, founded in 1963 / Member of The Claremont Colleges, Claremont, California 91711

Bert Meyers

March 11, 1968

Dear Mr. Auden:

I asked Doubleday to send you a copy of my second book of poems, <u>The Dark Birds</u>, because I admire your work; also, because I met you one evening at the Gotham Book Mart in 1948, an occasion that still means a great deal to me. Edith Sitwell was there. I was nineteen, broke, shabby, nearly mad, living in a little room on 92nd and Columbus, reading Rilke, Hart Crane, and Thomas Mann. You were very kind. I bummed many cigarettes from you, your hands were orange with nicotine.

Now, you live at 77 St. Marks Place. I used to live there. My uncle, a doctor, owned the building then. He was a superb abortionist who made a fortune from his skill and died at the age of eighty nine in an old people's home. There used to be an Hungarian restaurant in the basement where my grandfather and I spent the evenings drinking turkish coffee. At two in the morning we'd push back the tables, my grandfather would play the piano, and the old ladies pulled up their skirts--the varicose veins on their fat legs glowing like neon--and danced until four.

Leon Trotsky had a room there, when he was in New York. The place was full of gypsies and Roumanian Jews. My grandfather often climbed down the fire escape at dawn, carrying a foetus wrapped in newspaper which he'd burn in the incinerator. My uncle knew eight languages fluently, but only changed his shirt twice a year.

So, I hope you enjoy the book. But if you dislike the poems, and have the time, I'd appreciate your telling me why.

With best wishes,

Bert Meyers

Bert writes a letter to Auden about once living in his same apartment, 1968.

Dear Saki,

Around 1912 modern poetry began with the imagists — Pound, H.D., etc. Imagist Poems were short, prosaic in diction, and free verse in form. Their style became formalized in Arthur Waley's translations from the Chinese, which were begun after 1916. The various styles in Pound's <u>Personae</u> (1912-1916) reflect a desire for models other than those found in the English language. The first great wave of translations from "modern" French poetry probably began in the latter half of the 19c with Swinburne and Symons — Baudelaire, Verlaine, Gautier, etc. Translations of Rimbaud and Breton, as well as Eluard, Michaux, Aragon, etc, began to appear during the 2nd World War. Generally speaking, the tone of American poetry between 1918 and 1950, let's say, was determined by Eliot and the New

(2)

Critics, ie, metaphysical, well-made, ironic, etc. Examples, aside from major poets, would be Tate, Ransom, Shapiro, Lowell, etc. After the 2nd World War poetry, like painting, become more international in style. American poets (some, that is) began looking for models outside the English tradition. Surrealism offered the best way of restoring the unconscious, the irrational image, a contemporary sense of reality, free verse, etc, to an honorable role in making poems. This process occured in other countries, eg, Turkey, China, Korea, Japan, Spain, Latin America, earlier than in the U.S. Except for Dylan Thomas, David Gascoyne, Edith Sitwell, etc, English poets haven't been influenced by Surrealism. In Germany, since 1945, poets are using a neo-surrealist style, combined with the expressionism that characterized their poetry

The start of a letter to Bert's dear friend Sacvan Bercovitch, who was an influential and controversial figure in American studies. In it, Bert responds to "Saki's" query on the history and lineage of Contemporary Poetry. Bert begins with Modernism.

Bert at his desk.

from a letter to Hugh Miller, June 26, 1972

...

Now, I'm convinced that the whole planet's a dynamic system and that man's a shabby yet glittering mirror, an engineer who duplicates nature endlessly. Love, first learned from our parents and community, has made our lives both noble & tragic. That's why I worship the eternal in the present. Why should I want to burn furiously, then desintegrate back into the mulch of events? I love my wife's face, my children, the tree in front of our house, an occasional handshake, the hours that pass like trucks full of people and oranges, too much to suddenly be disconnected like a hub cap going blind by the road. Once, my consciousness never existed. Now, it does. It's only one little window in the city of time. Yet, from it I can sing, weep, smile, throw a bomb or a bouquet....

Bert Meyers

Note:

this is from a letter he showed me before he sent it, and I asked if I could copy this passage.
there should be many letters from /to Hugh Miller, with much on American poetry, politics, life in general.

He used to speak like that, too, at times, most often with young people; throw metaphors away right and left.

Odette Meyers

An excerpt from a letter to Hugh Miller, 1972, with a note from Odette, Bert's wife.

“And he still dreamed of a style / so clear it could wash a face, / or make a dry mouth sing.” —from “The Poets.”

Everson Reading — he read an hour
long poem about his sex life, comparing
its ups and downs, etc, with the course
of a powerful river through the American
landscape ~ a bi-centennial event ~
the metaphysical fascism of ecological
lust orchestrated by a Hollywood
director who read Hopkins and Jeffers...
(religion, alliteration + rhythm)
What Shit!

1976

A Face, a whole neighborhood,
Can disappear like trash...

Since my father died,
my mother floats away
on her sofa, over the past,
Seven floors above the ground...

1972

I tried lots of women
Cards liquor and pool
now all I can say is
I was a damn fool

'76

I've been in the factory
I've worked in the shops...

I'm as glum as a flag
taken down from the mast

Bert responds to seeing the poet William Everson read. From Bert's journals, 1976.

"Man made like his roads, / with somewhere to go." —from "Stars Climb Girders of Light." *Photo by Seymour Linden, 1967.*

These Days

homage to Attila József

These days, everything's bad.
The future waits in a button.
No one plans, nobody says:
Three years from now . . .

Evening falls upon a porch;
bloody, black and white,
it opens like the paper.
Someone bursts into flames.

Winter, a grim warehouse,
delivers the wind.
An angry truck rattles by—
the inconsolable self,
strumming its gas pedal,
tuning up for the storm.

Lies! so many lies!
Windows malignant with things.
When at last the nail
strangles the hammer
and even the ant howls.

Then rifles, rockets—
"O what a time, what a time!"

And, like an old ideal,
the moon's been reached.
A few astonished flies
wrinkle the dust on its face.

Be like the rain
that wears a ragged coat
and finds a lamp
in the smallest stone
and sings for nothing
from street to street.

1979

All Around Me

All around me, butterflies,
ecstatic hinges,
hunt for the ideal door.
A cicada's ratchet
tightens a place in the yard.
Everything's warmed
by a wave from the tree.

A bird trickles like the tap.

And the dog just stands there,
looking down.
Run, sleep, she can't remember.
It's hard to be conscious.

From here, I can watch the freeway—
ants on a windowsill.
The skyline doodles, an airplane
seems to float like a fish.

Nearby, a factory smokes.
I'm one of its little ash-trays.
Suddenly, a dinosaur,
or Rome, will rise,
then crumble, in the cracks
on a ragged wall.

We do marvelous things
without knowing how,
like the chicken whose bronze shit
builds a shrine under its coop.

But, even so,
one gets depressed.
This morning, a field,
a flock of stones
asleep in its mist . . .
This world's painted
on a glass that has
to break.

I can still
pay the rent
and the roads aren't lined
with corpses yet.

1979

Suburban Dusk

One girl in a red dress leaves the shopping center with empty hands: and you believe in the future—you've seen a drop of blood flee from the luminous cells of a corpse.

But the sky slips a coin in the slot between two buildings. Lights go on. Distorted creatures appear. A car, like an angry heart, explodes.

And a vast erysipelas spreads over the hills. What can you do? Each night, the city becomes a butterfly, trembling in its oil.

1979

Pebble

Fragment
of the first chunk
Irregular moon
Perpetual cloud
The dust's blind eye
The mite's
crude planet
Durable friend
between the fingers
Destroyer
of giants
Something that grows
immense in a shoe
The boulder's crumb
The rock's
quiet child
The flower's
pure disciple
Wasteland's embryo
Despair's gray seed
Staunch member
in the brotherhood
of water polishers
Wisdom's jewel
The weed's
eternal fruit
The raindrop's tomb

1979

Old

Their children are gone;
almost everyone
they loved and half
of what they understood,
has disappeared.

But the door's still open,
the porch light's on;
a little wind at night
and they hear footsteps
when a few leaves fall.

1979

Homecoming

1.

My father was a tender man
whose blue eyes would overcast
by noon. Every dusk
he floated home
in the soiled wind of his clothes.

I flew to the ceiling in his arms.
The silverware sang
as he came to the table
and the bright room rolled
like a train that climbs
its ladder through the dark.

2.

His hands are cobwebs full of flies,
trembling in his lap.
They've locked him up with strangers,
because he drools too much;
and I imagine freeing him.

We'd go to a town that isn't there,
where everyone he cries for now
(wrapped in the bed's thick bandage)
would come to shake his hand.
He laughs. He lifts a child and grows.
He drinks and drinks the meadowlark,
he smooths a stone's gray hair . . .

But he stinks, he's a huge bib;
a loose scab, a rotten cornflake,
clings to his lip.

3.

There are mouths so cold
the salmon-colored tongue
leaps without a sound;
lonely ditches where a broken dove
mourns in the rubble of a face.

Men, at the mercy of their parts:
grime in the skull, despair
corroding the rainbows in their wires.

4.

My home was a watercolor
I left in the rain . . .

Tonight, the crickets ring and ring,
nobody answers;
the shadows of men are looking for blood.

Someone has stepped
on the classical face of the moon.

Dawn comes, a gradual
mountain range of ashes.

5.

The mockingbirds, those joyful books
that opened in the sky,
then closed their pages on a branch,
awake and go mad,
chewing the bones of their old songs;
and the flies, such tiny fenders,
batter themselves in the air.

1979

Lament

1.

I looked for you at the cemetery.
You have two addresses
on a metal door in the grass;
but you don't live at either one.

2.

When I was a child
and sick at night,
you were the moon
above my bed.

Father, father,
I saw you smile
at a sparrow
the way you smiled at me.

3.

What else awakes and knows
it was born, it will die.
The same clouds come and go;
the same bird sings or flies.

1979

Driving Home at Night with My Children After Their Grandfather's Funeral

See how the moon follows us?
That's Grandpa's face in the sky.
It smiles; so, he's still the same.
Sleep. The way home's always
shorter than the way you came.

Shh . . . the car's a steel measure
that swallows the road like a tape;
and we'll all live twice as long
as it takes the snail to go
around the world on its crumpled skate.

1979

With Animals

1.

I feel like the elephant
enlightened boulder
held back by a chain

2.

I act like the camel
with its melancholy
sensual eyes
and fastidious lips

3.

I see the dung-colored
crumbling bison
an entire town evicted
even its sofas
falling apart
The young look over the fence
their eyes are maple leaves
after the rain
American lakes
a hundred years ago
Their mothers stare at the ground
their fathers shrink
like the countryside
The moon the oldest streetlight
touches them
with its intangible snow

4.

I envy the tortoise
primordial hand
whose neck is a thumb
measuring time and the grass

5.

I understand the stork
the way it paces
scholar or wandering Jew
whoever waits
for the real world to be born

6.

I want to comfort the ostrich
that mad woman
wearing her grandmother's clothes
and be like the mountain goats
who lick each other's forehead

7.

But look at the huge green toad
sanctimonious phlegm
The crocodile hell's pavement
Bats those weird umbrellas
that open only at night

8.

The baboon sulks on a shelf
prehistoric priest
whose rump is a festival
its face a sports car
his eyes glum headlights that glare

9.

There's that insect
winding itself again
another ant
berserk on its boulevard

10.

And somewhere a field mouse
sits by the sea

1979

I Can't Sleep

I can't sleep.
I wish we were young,
in a different house,
in a different town.
I can hear the dog
run away in her dream;
outside, raindrops—
their tender hoofbeats
trapped in the courtyard
of a leaf.

1976

And Still

Nobody's honest
nothing matters

That's why I'm always
adjusting myself
my chemicals
my complaints

And every day
I fly around
in my insect-colored car
The city's a carcass
streets quiver like meat

In my own voice
I hear a broom
that sighs while it waves
farewell to the past

And still it happens
a few leaves
come around a corner
demonstrate
then disappear
Mozart arrives
in an ice-cream truck
a long war ends
I feel like a streetlight

tall and radiant
my face was made
to shine among the others

1979

A Citizen

1.

The spider I hit,
loose thread on the floor,
clenches its fist.
The cat lies down;
it looks at me
as if through a window.

2.

I'm a coat hanger
twisted by rage.

3.

Everything shrinks from my hands—
that landscape threatened by planes,
a woman's astonished face.

4.

I served the giant
who ate the villages,
whose arms swept aside
the stars like raindrops
on a windshield;
who broke the sky,
man's sacred mirror,
and promised peace . . .

5.

I did these things for freedom,
endless as a boulevard
where all the lights are green.

6.

My car won't start.
Dead leaves follow me—
they're scribbling my name.

7.

I'm a swastika, the headless man
whose iron limbs grind the world.

8.

I want to change.
Even a wall gets painted again.

1979

Gently, Gently

We, too, began with joy.
Then, sickness came;
then, poverty.
We were poor, so poor,
our children were our only friends.

Gently, gently,
through anger and pain,
love justified itself,
like the nails in the house
during a storm.

Somehow, we created hope,
reliable drum
in the shadow's wrist;
a tuning fork
on the sidewalk of dreams.

At night, I was the one
who became a cello,
strung with all our roads,
where memory hums
to itself like a tire.

And you, mad as a clarinet
where the street divides;
a city of raindrops in a bush;
the slow honey that drips
from the sky's old ladle . . .

the reason I'm frightened of death.
I swear by the wings
love spreads at my waist,
that I'll carry your tune
until my tired strings break.

1979

Daybreak

Birds drip from the trees.
The moon's a little goat
over there on the hill;
dawn, as blue as her milk,
fills the sky's tin pail.

The air's so cold a gas station
glitters in an ice cube.
The freeway hums like a pipe
when the water's on.
Streetlights turn off their dew.

The sun climbs down from a roof,
stops by a house and strikes
its long match on a wall,
takes out a ring of brass keys
and opens every door.

1979

Bert and his wife Odette in 1976.

CERTIFICATE OF MARRIAGE

On Sunday, October 20th, 1957, the day had some wind, some rain and some sunshine. On the afternoon of this day, after placing half of their books away, Bert Meyers and Odette Miller read some poetry aloud to each other, then maintained one full minute of silence while looking at each other. Breaking the silence, they slipped the wedding bands on each other's finger, then broke bread with salt together and drank salted wine. After which, having as witnesses Walt Whitman and Olive Schreiner, they signed this certificate, thereafter consuming their marriage, and acting out their love in every gesture they made to each other and the world, every new thing they learned, and every new world they wrote.

Bert Meyers   Odette Sarah Miller

and

are now

Bertram Isaac Meyers

Odette Sarah Meyers

Marriage certificate handwritten by Bert, 1957.

A drawing by Bert for Odette after 15 years of marriage.

Bert, Odette, Daniel and Anat on the porch of their home, 1967.
Photo by Seymour Linden.

BERT MEYERS, MY FATHER: A MEMOIR

Daniel Meyers

In one of my earliest memories, my father was in the hospital. I was four years old. He was very sick with a lung disease that, though life threatening, he would recover from until eventually dying of lung cancer 14 years later. I didn't really know what death was, but when I arrived at the hospital and was brought into the room with my father, I vaguely understood that I could lose this man I loved so dearly. I was left alone to visit with him. He was in a surprisingly good mood and was sitting propped up in bed with a number of hospital pillows behind him and looking up at a small TV set mounted high on the wall. He was very excited and waved for me to come up and join him on the bed. He explained that a very important film was about to be shown on the TV.

I sat on the bed with my father's arm around my shoulder and I was happy, the anxiety of the setting having dissipated. On the little screen appeared *Nanook of the North*, the 1922 documentary by Robert Flaherty about the passing way of Eskimo life; a film, ironically, which was less of a documentary and more of an acted reconstruction. But I was mesmerized, and this memory still stands out as among the most immediate and visceral of my early childhood.

I watched Nanook on the black and white screen going about daily tasks. And then he started to build an igloo with his "family." As they constructed it, finishing it by cutting an opening to the igloo and crafting a window made out of ice, I sat transfixed.

At home there was a children's book of people's homes all around the world with drawings of an Eskimo and their igloo . . . and here I was seeing one being built by real people. I can still remember feeling that the people who had made this film had done something magical: not only had they shown me and my father something of the life of people far away, but these people, who were no longer alive, had been immortalized. With my father beside me, in his own precarious life and death situation, I felt greatly comforted by this film and decided then that one day I too would make films like this.

My father was one of those people in life—the artists, inventors, builders, writers—who leave something of their own being behind. Bert's passionate and deep experience of the real world—much better described by all the fine essays in this volume than by me, who is not a writer—resonates with people who want to find that same connection in a natural world that seems to be falling apart around us.

My sister Anat, my mother Odette and I lived together with this complex and difficult man, loving him, enduring him. And especially for my mother, who was his creative muse and a writer herself, and for my sister and me as well, his poetry was like another member of the family. We heard the poems grow up, evolve, revised, until they were shared with the rest of the world. His poetry had an enormous presence in our lives; we knew the images he described, the places he spoke of. Today, long after he has died, his poems still read to my sister and me like a hologram of him, of his being and experience of the world.

Bert Meyers was an intense man, a description all who knew him would agree with. I feared my father: his moods, his anger, his judgement. I respected his wealth of self-taught knowledge and well-earned strong opinions. And I was drawn like so many to his passion, his energy, his wildness. But above all I loved and admired him, and I appreciated all the time he would spend with me.

For better or for worse, he transmitted to me his fierce independence and desire to pave one's own way free of the constraints of convention. And he thought I could learn more out of school than inside it, like he himself did. He let me skip many days of school over many years. All I had to do was tell him what I was planning to do with my time, in a household with no TV. Riding my bike all around town with our family dog Lila, trying to build some crazy idea in my head, or reading one of the many great books he gave me, were all valid reasons to skip school.

But much of the time I spent my days hanging out with him: reading together, playing chess, him teaching me how to make gold leaf frames, taking long walks with Lila, observing the world and talking of everything. We drove into downtown L.A. and watched wild kung fu movies with flying and magic and those early but wonderful low quality special effects. Afterwards we would sit in a café and watch people walk by, taking turns telling each other what we imagined they were doing, thinking, where they were coming from or where they were going in their lives. I knew no father who spent as much time with his son. All these precious moments live, like his poetry, with me to this day.

Postcards

For Odette

Ocean

There it is: an immense, gray, agitated circle . . .

and all day long the boat goes on
like a cartridge across a turntable,
an old shoe in a storm,
dipping itself in the spume.

***

If the sun shines, the water grinds its glass.

***

When calm, the sea's so blue
you could paint the sky with it.
Sometimes, it's a green tablecloth
laid on the wind.

Fog—
sailing for hours
in the same spot;

and the joyful sound
of the invisible sea.

***

On the horizon, late at night,
a ship glows like the last café
still open
at the end of a boulevard
after the rain.

Island

Dwarfs and hunchbacks
are loading wagons.
Gardens drip in the heat.
Flowers burst from the walls.
An ox appears
like a hillside in an alley.

***

At the grocery store,
chamber pots display their bottoms
from the rafters,
chicks lament among the onions . . .
So poor, a box
of baking soda's
smaller than a cigarette pack.

***

A group of boys, in double file,
marches down a street.
A young, skinny priest, a scorched twig,
walks behind them, reading Scripture.
Pale girls lean on their windowsills,
framed like the earliest photographs.

***

Passengers board the ship at twilight.
The people who wave from the pier
light matches—they become
a crowd of candles on the shore.
The boat, a huge altar, dissolves in the fog.

Arrival

Two sailboats cross the bay,
as if the wind wore tennis shoes.

***

Villages, like broken pots,
or baskets of apples,
scattered on a mountainside.

***

And the light, so much light!
a harp burning in a glass.

Village

A farmer swings a scythe,
tilting the blade's sharp edge.
The weeds are waves that fall
on a glistening coastline.
When he stands it up,
the scythe's a tall, one-legged bird,
whose long bill the farmer cleans.

***

The cemetery's such a pretty town—
old, quiet, full of mansions.
People, flowers, crows, everyone comes.

***

A market in the street.
Herbs, those quiet housewives,
wearing their modest prints,
were found in the fields at dawn.
Clods of garlic, the kitchen's diamond,
hang from every stall.
Cheese, like the walls of France;
red peppers with a plastic glow . . .

***

The cook speaks softly, gesturing,
as if she were washing her hands in French.
She loves to look at the sea
when the water ripples
and a gaggle of rowboats
wobbles near the shore.
She talks to the chickens in the garden.
They're very intelligent, she says . . .
they'd tell us beautiful stories
if they weren't so busy eating.

***

Frogs croak twenty-one in French all night.

***

In the morning, calves
stare at the world
with their mother's eyes.
The rabbits quiver—
they know so much
about freedom, death.

***

Inside the moldy church
you're wrapped in a damp rag.
A Christ, as smooth as soap,

hangs from a cross
near the entrance.
A bland virgin
in a faded blue robe
gestures from a niche.

***

Outdoors, a breeze
makes all the shrubs
look sociable.
White butterflies in a field
are the frayed handkerchiefs of those
who didn't finish saying good-bye.

Train

Sunlight plays its flute in the treetops.

***

A village where a church,
with one arm raised to the sky,
sinks in a cauldron of tiles . . .

and a castle whose towers rise
like a charred town
from the murky water of its walls.

***

Train station.
Empty platform,
not even a cat.
A flock of bells
crosses the tracks.

***

Green keeps changing itself from green to green.

Paris

City, where every wall's a canvas
(a torn poster's an allegorical town)
and time goes around painting the past . . .
Night lifts the moon like a coffee cup
from the skyline's cluttered shelf.
Each day, spring comes in the middle of fall.
Neighborhoods are history books,
leather-bound and stacked in their centuries.

***

In a little square, a man
fills a bottle at a fountain.
The sound of water stops, continues.
A woman leans from a window
to see how the sky feels.
Clouds rub their silver polish over the sun.

* * *

And here are also filthy streets,
leprous walls that sunlight
never touched, smeared with crud,
battered like garbage cans . . .
the cracks in a stone
are a landscape of nerves;
the air's a perpetual fart
and even the shadows wear rags.

* * *

An old dog, a four-legged
bundle of straw,
leaves the café and goes
to the gutter for a drink.
When he returns, his footprints
are a crooked row
of tiny vases, each one
with four flowers, on the sidewalk.

* * *

A child carries a long,
thin loaf of bread.
Its sides are chipped
like the molding of a gilded frame.
The crust looks warm, dented,
as if the baker were a blacksmith
who hammered and sold the sun's rays.

Jardin du Luxembourg

Birds, in their brown suits,
hurry home from business.
Clouds lie rumpled in the sky
like napkins after dinner.
A chandelier of rain hangs over the lake.

The queens of France are always here.
Their poignant pride endures
the casual gaze of foreigners,
the pigeons and the years.

Arc de Triomphe

Nothing but gray seen through the arch—
as if triumph were an abyss
into which a nation marches.

14th of July

Fireworks—an empire's crown
that lasts for a moment.

A tough guy shows a timid girl
how to dance in the street.

Buttes-Chaumont

From this melancholy cliff
the park unrolls,
a thick green mist below . . .

And Paris, like a sea
without its water—
the world's most delicate
accumulation of debris.

***

Some days are harpsichords
under the chestnut trees.
Nothing lasts, their strings break,
the gold turns gray, a drizzle falls . . .
And then the gold's restored.
People leave their tables,
birds their narrow benches in the walls.
An old woman sits and bathes
her tired feet that look like marble
in a puddle near the market stalls.

***

Among the antique dealers,
a pigeon on the sidewalk's
a little baron who struts
through a village of bric-a-brac.

***

It rained and rained in the courtyard
and an old man in a gray coat
sang to empty windows.
The laundry wept for hours.

***

The round slate roofs of grand hotels,
mythical in their scales,
float through the radiant water of the air.
But the buildings of the poor
divide their bread with everyone.
At night, each window's a glass of wine
the darkness drinks as it passes.

***

Sometimes, a blind violinist
helps us through the street.
You shed a few coins in his cup—
a shop front glitters
like an accordion in the rain.

***

Cars whirl around a monument.
People smile, horns blare,
headlights shine like brass.
The whole square's a carousel.
Suddenly, you're a child
who's had his turn, a stranger;
the others stay, but you go home.

***

Now, from the dawn's gray chemical,
a café's a postcard in the distance . . .
a barge strolls through Paris on the Seine . . .

1979

BE LIKE THE RAIN: A MEMOIR

Ari Sherman

A former teacher of mine first told me of Bert Meyers, Pitzer and the Claremont Colleges. She felt I belonged at Pitzer, her alma mater, and got in touch with Admissions and several faculty members, including Bert, asking them to review my application. Soon after I was accepted, I drove from L.A. to see the campus and bought two of Bert's books, getting my first taste of his work while perched on the bookstore steps. I was thrilled by how commonplace objects and imagery, much of it Southern Californian, became the building blocks of Bert's singular voice, a poetry so precise in word choice and so fluid in flow and leaps, I still find it daunting and delightful forty-three years later.

Starting college the following fall, I was anxious about fitting in. However, my first meeting with Bert set me at ease. He was both energetic and calm. He'd read my application and poems and pointed out key similarities in our life experience. We were both L.A. natives, creatures of concrete and chaparral, both actively leftist and culturally Jewish. Bert was acutely aware I'd been on my own since my father's death two years earlier. We touched on my travel experiences and a summer in Israel. He was pleased I counted international poets among my favorites and lent me books by Yannis Ritsos and Constantine Cavafy.

Our next meeting was a walk across campus and through town. We stopped at Pomona College to meet poets Robert Mezey and Dick Barnes who were excited about an upcoming reading, making clear my attendance was mandatory. Along the way he asked about my other classes and how I'd settled in. Bert's care for others, friends and students, showed in his insightful questions and close, attentive listening. Bert's poetry workshops exemplified this and his deep respect for writing itself; discussions of assigned poetry and student work were given equal weight.

After winter break, Bert was absent. He returned thinner and pale, tried to focus on teaching, but his illness was too much. On Bert's last visit to campus he used our final conversation unexpectedly, advising that while I should regard my year at Pitzer as proof I could succeed in college and was indeed becoming a poet, he'd prefer I leave school, travel, write, work, return to Israel, even visit Paris and Greece. He didn't mince words, saying he hated the thought of me returning to a Pitzer without him, only to be ensnared by grief. I hugged his thin frame gently as we parted.

We buried Bert in April as a chasm of loss enveloped us, rending an unhealable hole. His rangy striding form would be seen no more, and we were consoled only by what we'd learned from him. He taught that writing must come from truth and contain urgency. He believed in sharing work: in translation, readings, teaching and editing literary journals if possible—in other words, supporting our art. I still miss him.

The Poets

There he sat among them
(his old friends) a walking ash
that knows how to smile.
And he still dreamed of a style
so clear it could wash a face,
or make a dry mouth sing.
But they laughed, having found
themselves more astonishing.

They would drive their minds
prismatic, strange, each wrapped
in his own ecstatic wires,
over a cliff for language,
while he remained to raise
a few birds from a blank page.

1982

Public Places

In the small cafés the bars
the public places
you can be alone not lonely
your face is one among the faces
like an apple on an apple tree

You can sit there for an hour
you can sit there for a day
and plan the revolution
or like Shakespeare
write a tragic play
about your love and indecision
or watch the rain come down
and see the buildings float away

But you're not lonely here
just alone no need to fear
as long as you can pay
Light a cigarette and dream
time is an ocean not a stream
the voices rise and fall like waves
It's beautiful and sad to be alive
as all the ash-trays turn to graves

1982

Another Caterpillar Poem

for Robert Bly

As I lift the coffee cup I see a caterpillar crawl over the sheet of airmail stamps.

Its head is a microphone dragging its cord. Used pipe cleaner, so many little accordions open and close like a mountain range of exhausted joy.

I pick up the blood-colored sheet and the caterpillar undulates like smoke at the edge of a field, then rises—an electrician bewildered by wires, a man whose remote feet are anxious staples gripping the ground.

Should I speak now about wings and the flower's sexual glare?

I think it's November again. Leaves are the grand-parents of spring. I don't mind that I've failed at times.

The desperate summer sleeps in the shade. The sweet legs of the grass have gone away.

I see the earth's plain face, its wrinkled belly, the family loaf that rises under the moon.

The caterpillar dreams, dark lightning, on the desk.

1982

The Daughter

She won't believe she was born without wings.
Why can't I live in the ceiling?

The heart's a wagon one pulls, empties and fills,
from door to door . . .

Once, she put some blocks
and a few bricks in a hole
she dug, watered them, and said
I'm growing a house.

Today, she stuck a green branch in the ground.
Look, I've made a fountain!

The porch is her piano.
When I play on the steps,
our neighbors smile.
We're like the Family of Man.

At bedtime, shadows hang the world
inside a gray museum.
All the pictures grow dim in the sky.

Then, her face wanders on the pillow
like a flashlight in the dark.

1982

The Son

He arranged some rocks in circles on the rug.
These are nests for invisible birds.
The fly's my friend. How old is it?

Near the beach he sees the fog open a jar of vaseline
headlights fumble with their yellow spoons.
Frightened, he sails away in his mother's arms.

Tomorrow, he'll claim he didn't sleep all night
to make the sky,
I pinned up a blue cloth when I ran out of paint
and I used a dirty quilt for Chicago.

Death drives a man
like a nail into the ground;
his head turns to metal
and shines in the grass . . .

But here, at home,
when the morning washes my window,
time returns in a golden bus.
I want to ride as long as I can.

1982

Without a Chance

You were born
without a chance
and you don't stand
a chance tonight

You see eternity
come into sight
as that big shiny car
pulls up to the curb

Oh those are knives
not the headlights in the leaves
and something breaks your nerve
and then your knees

The moon looks down
and doesn't care
when your blood lights up
your pretty hair
You were born
without a chance
and you don't stand
a chance tonight

Eternity's as long
as the car
that pulls up to the curb
space opens at your feet

Everything gets blurred
the moon has a dirty face
the stars are broken glass
in a dark and empty street

1982

Maybe

(for Ami)

We love the sunlight on an old wall's broken face. Now and then, we want to lie around all afternoon in a personal cloud. At night, after a storm, we wake our children to show them the fragile city of raindrops in a tree.

We wish that one clear hour could last a year; that we could buy a dinner with our dreams and stroll out the door, past reality, down a street where everyone says, Hello.

We filled the moon and the stars and everything on earth with our desire; and still, life doesn't hum like a hedge in summer.

Well, maybe one by one we'll announce when it's time to dress in our ideal selves; then, celebrate the days that grow—fresh from the cleaners, the bakery, the pages of a brand new book.

Those beautiful days, those sensible days, almost everyone knew just had to come.

1982

Sunflowers

No one spoke to the sunflowers,
those antique microphones
in the vacant lot.
So, they hung their heads
and, slowly, fell apart.

1982

It's All Dissolving

It's all dissolving
like an aspirin
in a glass of doom

Speak quietly
there's a microphone
in every tree
and a White House on the moon

They've killed today
and put tomorrow
in a cage
and feed it
promises and lies

Sometimes you're glowing
with a silent rage
and broken bloodshot eyes
The unemployed are hungry
the boss plays in the snow

It's all dissolving
and there ain't no place to go
I felt a raindrop burn
I heard bones crumble in a breeze
Chemicals are everywhere
and everything's diseased

And the funerals drive by
with their headlights on at noon

through cancer's crazy city
where everyone dies too soon

But when the rich and mighty
were at their banquet
feeling safe and sound
blind Samson had a vision
and pulled the temple down

1982

Images

for Odette

I

Bales of hay—cartons
of sunlight fading in a field.

II

Shadows rise like water,
white fences comb their hair.

III

Leaves everywhere—
shreds of a giant eraser;
an oak leaf,
becoming an antique.

IV

Outside, a snowfall's passed
and painted all the windowsill,
even the curb's a gray putty.

V

Sunlight in a window—
a flower in a glass.

VI

The highway's an old
surrealist's granite hair;
and the sea's become
a sky full of clouds.
A wind records the waves,
then plays them in the trees.

VII

A flock of crows
dissolves in the mist—
a cigarette's ash
in a glass of water;
and sunlight
twitching in a puddle.

VIII

Now the night drives up.
Distant buildings are golden radiators,
the sky's a black cloud
full of sparks . . .
Sirens, dogs;
and he just stood there,
by the police car,
with those handcuffs on,
staring at the moon.

IX

After the rain
a streetlight hangs
the shadow of trees
like laundry
on a wall.

X

Hands, twin sisters
to whom everyone's
a wrinkle
that needs to be smoothed,
a stranger who should be fed.

Hands, those humble wings
that make each day
fly toward its goal;
at rest, still holding
the shape of a tool.

XI

Proletarian aristocrat
whose forehead glows
like imagination's egg;
when you're asleep
you look like
the death mask of Keats,
alone with yourself
again—absolute, relieved.

XII

I wish we were two birds
living in a courtyard
near St. Germain des Prés.
Leaves spread their tablecloths,
trees open their cafés;
all day the sun's a barrel of beer,
at night the earth's a woman,
the full moon's her mirror.

1982

POSTSCRIPTS

July 12/61

Dear Bert Meyers,

It isn't a habit with me to write fan letters, but I've just read your book *Early Rain* & would just like you to know it has given me more pleasure than just about any other new book I've read since *Heart's Needle*. It ain't *all* good, but it gave this reader the feeling it was all honest, which you can't say for too many poetry books these days. "On the Hill," "In Those Hills," "My Parents," "We Thank the Heart," "Legend," "Now It's Friday," and "At Work" were the ones that I liked especially — all good poems, and that many good poems in a book is a hell of a lot to be grateful for.

Yours,

X.J. Kennedy

Fan letter from American poet X.J. Kennedy to Bert, 1961.

To Whom It May Concern:

Many are the things that slip by in the harsh velocity of American experience. The work of Bert Meyers might have been one of them if we didn't have the timeless vitality of his words on paper. Bert Meyers was a poet and his poetry is pershaps some of the best written in America after World War II. That poetry possesses the combination of delicacy and grit that informs the national lyricism at its best.

Clutter was something Bert Meyers had no interest in, which makes his work as stark as the very best blues lyrics. He was elegantly refined but also tough enough to understand the tragedy that slashes the throat of innocence. So some of the poems have the smell and the stickiness of fine perfume and blood. But on another level there is the oddly grave and giddy sense of humor, the celebrations of the seasons and of the natural world, the tenderness that seems linked to a long memory of compassion and desire.

Bert Meyers was genuine and would not submit to trends. He couldn't submit to anything other than the music in his ears and that music's demand that he lift his hand and push melody onto paper, word by word, lyric by lyric, rhythm by rhythm. We are quite lucky that his work, in all its complexity, its mournful melancholy, and its unexpected celebration of living right on the lip of existence, didn't get lost in the howl and the speed of our cultural juggernaut.

Stanley Crouch

Letter from American critic Stanley Crouch on Bert's poetry, after Bert's death in 1979.

THE ONLY CLOUD IN TROUSERS: A MEMOIR

Barry Sanders

Bert Meyers, and not Vladimir Mayakovsky, was the true "Cloud in Trousers." For someone or something had blessed Bert with a shock of bright white and tightly curled hair—but "no grey hair in his soul," as the Russian put it—over which, almost always, even in the classroom, hovered a cumulonimbus of white cigarette smoke. Bert preferred Shermans—only the brown ones—because Nat Sherman's cigarettes, unlike those poisonous Lucky Strikes, or those foul Camels, were good for you. He said it with a straight face and I think he actually believed it—even after his cancer.

I first met Bert in 1971, at someone's house in Claremont, after my job talk at Pitzer. That was fifty years ago—over a lifetime ago, several lifetimes, it feels, since so many of our friends and colleagues—the majority of them writers—have passed away. At that reception, Bert walked up to me, without introducing himself—I had, of course, never seen him before—and, in his no-nonsense way, asked: "You're a literature person, so, of all the Romantics, who's your favorite?" He paused a single beat: "And do not say Wordsworth!" Then he took a long drag on a slim, brown cigarette, stared at me and, as if he were unburdening himself of all life's troubles, exhaled a tsunami of smoke, and slowly, his smirk became a wonderful smile.

I answered quickly, out of fear at getting the answer wrong but also my fear of dying inside that lethal fog. "John Clare," I said. "Great," he shot back. "I love so-called minor poets. No one pays much attention to Clare. He went mad, you know; spent the last years of his life locked up in an asylum." I had a different take on Clare and wondered if I should tell him: Bert seemed formidable, and also the possibility of my getting a full-time job was on the line. I said that a writer I liked very much, G. K. Chesterton, believed that poets never go mad. Only mathematicians lose their minds. For Chesterton, the only great poet who ever went truly mad was John Cowper, and that, too, was on account of numbers—because of the suffocating logic that drove his belief in predestination.

Bert looked puzzled, even disbelieving, but still interested. He took another drag on his cigarette, exhaled a dragonfull, nodded, and stared at me. I kept going: Chesterton claims that the hatter went mad, not from inhaling mercury vapors, but from measuring too many heads. Precise measurements drove the hatter straight to the asylum. The villain isn't words, but numbers.

Then I said, "What do *you* do? He answered, underscoring it with what I came to know as the well-known Meyers grin:

"I gather images. Some people say I'm a poet. My wife actually believes it. And, as far as I'm concerned, you've got the job."

I got the job. The year was 1972. Our offices were in the same building, down the hall from each other. I spent a good deal of time with Bert in his office, at his house, at the local pie shop (his favorite: strawberry rhubarb). We became fast friends. With some others at the college and in Claremont, we edited a poetry magazine for a time: *Grove: Poetry in Translation.* He lamented that there was no place on campus where "a person could just sit and gather images."

Seven short years later, in 1979, I would weep at his funeral trying to read one of his poems aloud. I weep even more today. What else to do when Bert warned us that the city was an ashtray? Yet I can still see him at that long ago party, walking to the front door after our conversation about British Romantics: a shock of grey hair, a cloud of grey smoke, a phenomenon. He waved goodbye and, just like a cloud, disappeared.

Bert in his early twenties.

FIRE UNDRESSED MY BONES: REMEMBERING POET BERT MEYERS

Maurya Simon

I had two reasons for enrolling in Pitzer College in 1978: to finally complete my B.A. and to study with poet Bert Meyers, whose poetry had knocked me off my feet. It had been nearly ten years since I'd been an undergrad at U.C. Berkeley, and returning to college as a twenty-seven-year-old mother of two small daughters made me feel ancient and out of my element on campus.

During our first day of class, Bert sat at the head of an oblong table in our seminar room, his white mane of hair leonine, and his striking blue eyes gazing at each of the eight students present with an intense curiosity. He asked us what we thought poetry was, and why did we want to write it? His voice was beautifully sonorous, rich and clear. A halo of cigarette smoke encircled Bert's somber face as students struggled to articulate their poetic aims. I stuttered out some quickly improvised answers, feeling that I'd already failed in his estimation. But he nodded sagely and then said, "The only reason to write poems is because you can't avoid writing them. There has to be some internal imperative driving each person to tackle this ancient art form." He paused, then added, "But God knows you'll never make a shekel from poetry."

Then he passed out mimeographed copies of his favorite poems—an eclectic array of French, Greek, Serbian and American poets. I'd not read any of these poems before, and each one was a revelation. Bert quietly read aloud to us Édouard Roditi's translation of Breton's "Freedom of Love," and I felt the hairs on my arms lift and my breath accelerate:

> My wife with the hair of a wood fire
> With the thoughts of heat lightning
> With the waist of an hourglass
> With the waist of an otter in the teeth of a tiger
> My wife with the lips of a cockade and
> of a bunch of stars of the last magnitude . . .

Bert talked about surrealism for a few minutes, sternly telling us that there was always a "strangely perfect logic" to surrealist poems, and that merely recording one's dreams or throwing a bunch of disparate and unrelated images together did *not* constitute a surreal poem. His manner was intimidating. It was clear that poetry was sacrosanct to him and that we needed to take it as seriously as nuclear war or heart surgery.

When our first seminar meeting ended an hour later, I was convinced that poetry could actually change the world—it could alter a person's apprehension of time and space, the perception of herself, and the possibilities inherent in being alive and mortal. There are so many ways that poetry expands a reader's inner geography, I thought walking out of Bert's classroom that day, my ears ringing and my mind vibrating with poetry.

Bert's poems enthralled me—their use of stunning metaphors, their poignancy and imagistic brilliance, and their lapidary perfection. His poems often offer fresh insights spun from mundane objects or perceptions, ranging expressively in breadth and depth. Sometimes they're playful, as when they depict animals ("bats those weird umbrellas / that open only at night"), for instance, or they may be bittersweet when they zero in on a domestic scene, or angry when they decry war or the existential angst the poet feels. A masterful imagist, Bert never simply portrays places, events, or objects; instead, he brings a trenchant pathos or sharp insight to them. In "The Garlic," Bert provides a deft description of a head of garlic, while also paying tribute to this condiment's culinary and domestic power:

> Rabbi of condiments,
> whose breath is a verb,
> wearing a thin beard
> and a white robe;
> you who are pale and small
> and shaped like a fist,
> a synagogue,
> bless our bitterness,
> transcend the kitchen
> to sweeten death— . . .

Though sometimes melancholy, Bert's poems also contain a deep reverence for the world's intrinsic beauty, and his highly original and striking metaphors force readers to see even the simplest things anew, as evidenced by these lines from the remarkable poem "Pebble," one of my favorites:

> Fragment
> of the first chunk
> Irregular moon
> Perpetual cloud
> The dust's blind eye
> The mite's
> crude planet
> Durable friend
> between the fingers
> Destroyer
> of giants . . .

Taking Bert's class was a great gift, even though I often felt dumbstruck and fearful as I sat just a few feet from him. He could be quite scornful of students' poems, and of their lazy reading and writing habits. I'd seen my fellow classmates wince, go pale, or shudder almost imperceptibly when Bert critiqued their poems, doing so with tact, but also with an unsparing honesty. So I said little and absorbed everything he said, rushing off after each class session to Honnold Library to devour poetry volumes written by a moveable feast of international writers whom Bert admired, among them Chilean poet-diplomats Pablo Neruda and Gabriela Mistral, Russian poet Osip Mandelstam, Hungarian poet Attila József, Polish poets Anna Swir and Wisława Szymborska, and Spanish poet Gloria Fuertes.

I was too shy to visit Bert during office hours, but I longed to discuss my outside reading with him. I felt exhilarated and deeply moved by the rousing poetry to which he'd introduced me. One day, mid-semester, he asked me to go to his office after class. Initially filled with trepidation, I was relieved and surprised when Bert plied me with some poetry books from his personal library, urging me to read them. Then he said, "You don't say much in class, but it's clear that you think like a poet." He paused while I blushed, then he added rather bitterly, "It's not a vocation I'd encourage anyone to follow, but in your case, maybe you should keep at it." He combed his long, slender fingers through his white curls, fixing me with an intent stare, then added, "You've got the keen ear and stubborn heart of a poet. Clearly, nothing I say will dissuade you from it." I'd secretly hoped for just such a validation from Bert, yet I never actually expected to hear it. Even his ambivalent affirmation dazed and buoyed me.

At semester's end, I signed up for Bert's next poetry workshop. Following his tempered praise, I felt less insecure about showing him and our workshop members my poems. During one workshop, when another student suggested that a metaphor I used in my poem was "tired and clichéd," Bert exclaimed to me, "Be on guard!" Puzzled, I looked up at him inquiringly, and he added, "Don't let your language go slack and without purpose. Let it be an engine for perception, a testing ground for truth, and a finite lens to the infinite." Bert stared at me intensely, all the color drained from his face. His fiercely eloquent outburst reminded me that, for him, poetry was something intrinsically sacred and indispensable, and nothing less than the highest art form.

Midway through the following semester, Bert took me aside before class and said, "I'm quite ill and I don't know if I've got the energy to teach next week, or the week after. Would you serve in my place?" Stunned by his admission,

I said nothing for a moment, then—both mortified and honored—I agreed. The final stanza from Bert's poem, "After the Meal," haunted me during those weeks:

> Smoke waters the flowers
> that grow in the lungs.
> The cigarette, like your life,
> is a piece of chalk
> that shrinks as it tries to explain.

After Bert returned to class, ashen and emaciated, he invited me over to dinner at his house in Claremont Village, where I'd meet his wife Odette and his teenage children, Anat and Daniel. While Odette busied herself in their kitchen, she described her difficult childhood during World War II, speaking with a lilting French accent, and sometimes pausing to search for the best word or phrase in English. Nearly twenty years later, she'd publish her extraordinary memoir, *Doors to Madame Marie*, documenting her and her mother's survival as Jews living in Nazi-occupied France, and paying homage to her savior and mentor, Madame Marie Chotel.

After listening to Odette's fraught memories, and as I helped her set the dining room table, I glanced at the Meyers' refrigerator. It had several quotations pinned by magnets to it, and most of the comments focused on the same subject, mediocrity. I remember a few of those maxims: "Idleness is fatal only to the mediocre," from Albert Camus and "The only sin is mediocrity," from Martha Graham. But the one I found most memorable, due to its humor, was by novelist Joseph Heller: "Some men are born mediocre, some men achieve mediocrity, and some men have mediocrity thrust upon them." The quotation sardonically parodies Shakespeare's famous lines from *Twelfth Night*, and it reminded me how once, in class, Bert had railed against mediocrity in poetry, saying that it was "the worst offense in art."

As we ate, I noticed how Bert merely pushed his food around on his plate, eating little, while the rest of us hungrily devoured our meals. He looked so frail it was alarming, yet he was kind and solicitous, asking me a bevy of questions about my time living in India, my family, and my literary heroes and heroines. As we cleared our plates, and Bert returned to his armchair reading, Odette mentioned that she typed all of Bert's poetry drafts for him. Her comment startled me, since I couldn't imagine my husband doing the same for me, nor would I have tolerated him standing at my elbow while I penned revisions. I was genuinely surprised that Odette, also a poet, as well as a translator and professor of French literature at the Claremont Colleges, served as Bert's secretary. I wondered if she acted as Bert's aesthetic collaborator, as well as his scribe—an intriguing prospect.

I never asked Odette this question, for Bert died a month or so later, and though I remained friends with her over the ensuing years, my question was no longer relevant. I was crushed by Bert's death, dazed by the finality and cruelty of his loss. The students in our poetry workshop were also bereft, and though we continued meeting weekly without our mentor, a heavy pall hung over us. It was as if the sun had vanished and we were left in utter darkness, dazed and adrift.

I was touched and grateful when Barry Sanders, another Pitzer College professor and mentor, invited me to drive with him and his wife Grace to Bert's funeral in Los Angeles. I squeezed into the back seat of Barry's station wagon, crowding alongside two of his colleagues, film critic Beverle Houston and philosophy professor Jim Bogen. While we drove, I listened to Bert's friends relate affectionate and funny anecdotes about him, realizing how much he was loved and admired by them.

Although I don't remember the chapel where Bert's funeral was held, I do recall how moved I was by the simple eloquence of Bert's plain pine coffin—unadorned, as is the Jewish custom, and placed on a plinth. I knew that he'd have appreciated the craftsmanship and care that went into the making of his modest and austere casket. I cried through his friends' and colleagues' impassioned eulogies and was further saddened by seeing Odette's and her kids' distraught, sorrowful faces. Robert Mezey, a Pomona College poet and close friend of Bert's, wept as he helped Barry, Jim Bogen, and Daniel Meyers carry the coffin out of the chapel at the close of the service. It seemed inconceivable that so few of us were gathered in the chapel to bid farewell to Bert. How could such a monumental poet leave the world behind, without nations falling to their knees, and the earth halting in its rotation?

After we drove back to Claremont, I sat with my professors at Yianni's, a Greek café, where we toasted Bert with glasses of ouzo. Someone had brought a sheaf of Bert's poems, and we took turns reading them. Jim Bogen read Bert's poem, "The Dark Birds," with its concise rhyming couplets that are reminiscent of a nursery rhyme and its mysterious ending:

> . . . Then as I felt the birds return
> to me like ashes to an urn,
>
> and sunlight warmed the stones,
> fire undressed my bones.

Bert worked for ten years as a master picture framer and gilder until 1963, when his health was terribly impacted by the work. This still is from a commercial photo shoot to promote one of the Los Angeles galleries for which Bert worked.

AFTERWORD

Daniel Meyers

The story of this Unsung Masters book, published forty-four years after my father's death, and the story of *In a Dybbuk's Raincoat*, his collected works published twenty-eight years after his death, is the story of my father's poetry and soul living far beyond his far too short life.

It's also the story of the many people who helped in this journey. First and foremost is my mother, Odette. From the year my father died in 1979 to the end of her life in 2001, she tried to get my father's collected works published. One of the people with whom Odette was in regular contact in her search for a publisher was the late poet Morton Marcus. After Odette's death, he continued those efforts and the collected works, *In a Dybbuk's Raincoat*, finally found its home at the University of New Mexico Press Poetry Series in 2007, edited by Mort and myself. The fact that Bert's work has been remembered this long owes a great deal to Mort.

But there is another important side to who my father was, besides being a poet.

Bert Meyers was a teacher, the kind of teacher who marks and influences their students for a lifetime. Three in particular have formed an informal but crucial support group for me and the efforts to keep Bert's poetry read and available. Without the regular conversations, exchange of ideas, and all the support of Amy Gerstler, Garrett Hongo, and Maurya Simon, I may not have had the courage to continue.

I met another "student" of Bert's in 2007 when I had the pleasure of doing a reading with Dana Levin to promote the release of Bert's collected works. In 1984, Dana had arrived at Pitzer College, where my father had taught for eleven years until his death in 1979. While Dana was not a student of Bert's in his lifetime, she discovered and was greatly inspired by his work during her stay at Pitzer. Now, as the main editor of this Unsung Masters volume, Dana, co-editor Adele Elise Williams, and publisher Kevin Prufer, are helping to bring my father's work to yet another generation of people. With this Unsung Masters volume, Bert Meyers' poetry can be read and heard anew.

And to preserve the work by and about my father, far beyond the books that can go in and (mostly) out of print, I am creating the website bertmeyers.com, which will house all his poetry and prose, published and unpublished, audio and filmed recordings of him reading, as well as filmed interviews I conducted with old friends of his, including Magnum Photos photographer Elliott Erwitt and the writer and critic Stanley Crouch. I hope you enjoy it.

INDICES AND CREDITS

INDEX OF EPHEMERA: PHOTOS, DOCUMENTS, AND DRAWINGS

INDEX OF ESSAYS

JOSÉ ANGEL ARAGUZ, PH.D. is the author of *Rotura* (Black Lawrence Press, 2022). His poetry and prose have appeared in *Prairie Schooner, Poetry International, The Acentos Review,* and *Oxidant | Engine* among other places. He is an Assistant Professor at Suffolk University where he serves as Editor-in-Chief of *Salamander* and is also a faculty member of the Solstice Low-Residency MFA Program. He blogs and reviews books at *The Friday Influence.*

JIM BOGEN was a colleague of Bert's at Pitzer College from 1967 until Bert's death in 1979. He taught philosophy at Pitzer until retiring and moving to Pittsburgh, where he was a fellow of the Center for Philosophy of Science at the University of Pittsburgh, serving as an adjunct professor in the Department of History and Philosophy of Science. His interests include ancient Greek philosophy, Wittgenstein, epistemology of science, and topics in the history and philosophy of neurosciences. He is the author of many works of philosophy, including *Saving the Phenomena* (with Jim Woodward), *Observations, Theories and the Evolution of the Human Spirit* (with Jim Woodward), and *Aristotle on Motion, Change, and Contrariety* (with J.E. Mcguire).

VICTORIA CHANG'S forthcoming book of poems, *With My Back to the World,* will be published in 2024 by Farrar, Straus & Giroux. Her latest book of poetry is *The Trees Witness Everything* (Copper Canyon Press, 2022). Her nonfiction book, *Dear Memory* (Milkweed Editions), was published in 2021. *OBIT* (Copper Canyon Press, 2020), her prior book of poems, was named a *New York Times Notable Book*, a *Time Must-Read Book,* and received the *Los Angeles Times* Book Prize, the Anisfield-Wolf Book Award in Poetry, and the PEN/Voelcker Award. It was also longlisted for a National Book Award and named a finalist for the National Book Critics Circle Award and the Griffin International Poetry Prize. Chang has received a Guggenheim Fellowship, and served as the 2022 Poetry Editor for the *New York Times Magazine.* She lives in Los Angeles, where she is the Acting Program Chair and faculty member within Antioch's low-residency MFA Program.

AMY GERSTLER considers herself wildly lucky to have been a student of Bert Meyers' at Pitzer College in the late 1970s. She has published 13 books of poetry, most recently *Index of Women* (Penguin Random House, 2021). Her work has appeared in a variety of magazines and anthologies, including the *New Yorker* and *Paris Review.* She is currently collaborating with composer, actor, and arranger Steve Gunderson on a musical play. Her previous books of poems include *Scattered at Sea, Dearest Creature, Ghost Girl,*

Medicine, Crown of Weeds, Nerve Storm, and *Bitter Angel.* In 2019, she received a Foundation for Contemporary Arts C.D. Wright Award. In 2018, she was awarded a Guggenheim Fellowship. Gerstler has also written fiction, nonfiction, and journalism and art criticism.

HONGO, GARRETT

Poet, memoirist, and audio writer GARRETT HONGO studied poetry under Bert Meyers at Pitzer College from 1971-73. Hongo was born in Volcano, Hawai'i and grew up there and in Los Angeles. His poetry collections are *Yellow Light* (1982), *The River of Heaven* (1988), which received the Lamont Poetry Prize and was a Finalist for the Pulitzer Prize, and *Coral Road* (2011). His most recent publication is *The Perfect Sound: A Memoir in Stereo* (2022). In other non-fiction, he has published *The Mirror Diary* (2017) and *Volcano: A Memoir of Hawai'i* (1995), perhaps his best known work. He has been recognized with fellowships from the Guggenheim Foundation, the Rockefeller Foundation, the Fulbright Program, and the National Endowment for the Arts. This year, he was given the Aiken Taylor Award for lifetime achievement in poetry. He lives in Eugene where he is Distinguished Professor of Creative Writing at the University of Oregon.

DANA LEVIN studied under Bert's spirit while at Pitzer College from 1984-1987. She is the author of five collections of poetry, all from Copper Canyon Press: *In the Surgical Theatre*, chosen by Louise Glück for the 1999 American Poetry Review/Honickman First Book Prize; *Wedding Day* (2005); *Sky Burial* (2011); *Banana Palace* (2016); and *Now Do You Know Where You Are* (2022), a New York Times Notable Book and Lannan Literary Selection. Levin is a grateful recipient of honors from the National Endowment for the Arts, PEN, the Library of Congress, as well as from the Rona Jaffe, Whiting, and Guggenheim Foundations. She serves as Distinguished Writer in Residence at Maryville University in Saint Louis.

Bert and Odette Meyers had two children: Anat Silvera, a jewelry designer and teacher at Silvera Jewelry School in Berkeley, California, and DANIEL MEYERS, a documentary director, cameraman and teacher based in Paris, France. Daniel has traveled all over the world making public television documentaries primarily for the BBC and other European TV networks, as well as creating documentary training programs for journalists and film students.

SANDERS, BARRY

BARRY SANDERS was Bert's colleague at Pitzer College, where he taught, among other things, the history of ideas and medieval church iconography. His projects occur increasingly at the intersection of art and activism, and include *The Green Zone: The Environmental Costs of Militarism*, which Project Censored named one of the top-ten censored stories of 2009, and "Over These Prison Walls," which invites collaborations between artists and incarcerated youth. He has twice been a finalist for the Pulitzer Prize and is the author of fourteen books, including *Sudden Glory: Laughter as Subversive History* and *Alienable Rights: The Exclusion of African-Americans in a White-Man's Land, 1619–2000* (with Francis Adams), winner of the Robert F. Kennedy Human Rights Award. He co-founded and chaired the M.A. in Critical Theory and Creative Research program at Pacific Northwest College of Art, where he taught for close to a decade. He is the Founding Executive Co-Director for the Oregon Institute for Creative Research.

SHERMAN, ARI

A former student of Bert Meyers, ARI (LAURENCE) SHERMAN is a graduate of Pitzer College, a recipient of a Thomas J. Watson Fellowship, and holds a master's degree from the Creative Writing Program at the University of California Davis. Following his studies, he taught college for several years (Pitzer College, Mount San Antonio Community College, and Cal State Northridge) before transitioning into advertising. For over thirty years he has had a career writing advertising campaigns for major motion pictures and TV series as well as advertising and content for other sectors and major non-profits. And yes, he still writes poetry.

SIMON, MAURYA

MAURYA SIMON was a student of Bert Meyers at Pitzer College from 1978-79. She's the author of ten volumes of poetry, including, *The Wilderness: New and Selected Poems*, which was awarded the 2019 Gold Medal from the Independent Booksellers Association. Her poems have been translated into French, Hebrew, Greek, Farsi, and Spanish. She's received a Fulbright Senior Research Fellowship (Bangalore, South India), an NEA Fellowship in Poetry, as well as the Lucille Medwick and Cecil Hemley Memorial Awards from the Poetry Society of America. She's been a Visiting Writer at the American Academy in Rome, the Baltic Centre for Writers & Translators (Sweden), Hawthornden Castle (Scotland), and the MacDowell Colony. Simon serves as a Professor of the Graduate Division and Professor Emerita at the University of California, Riverside and lives in the San Gabriel Mountains of southern California.

SINGER, SEAN

SEAN SINGER is the author of *Discography* (Yale University Press, 2002), winner of the Yale Series of Younger Poets Prize, selected by W.S. Merwin, and the Norma Farber First Book Award from the

Poetry Society of America; *Honey & Smoke* (Eyewear Publishing, 2015); and *Today in the Taxi* (Tupelo Press, 2022). He runs a manuscript consultation service at www.seansingerpoetry.com.

WILLIAMS, ADELE ELISE

ADELE ELISE WILLIAMS is a writer, editor and educator. She is a PhD candidate in Literature and Creative Writing at The University of Houston where she serves as Nonfiction Editor for *Gulf Coast.* Adele is a finalist for *The Georgia Review's* 2022 Loraine Williams Poetry Prize and the winner of the Emily Morrison Poetry Prize and Inprint Donald Barthelme Prize for Poetry as well as the recipient of fellowships from UCROSS, Inprint, and Hindman Settlement School. Adele's work can be found in *The Georgia Review, Crazyhorse, Guernica, Cream City Review, The Florida Review, The Adroit Journal, Beloit Poetry Journal,* and elsewhere.

INDEX OF POEMS

CREDITS

Copper Nickel: Poems by Bert Meyers: "And Still," "At Night," "Funeral," "The Poet," "Some Definitions at Work"

Literary Matters: "Fire Undressed My Bones: Remembering Poet Bert Meyers" by Maurya Simon.

Poetry Magazine "On Bert Meyers" by Dana Levin. "A Gardener in Paradise" by Amy Gerstler. Poems by Bert Meyers: "Signature," "They Who Waste Me," "The Dark Birds," "Madman Songs," "Stars Climb Girders of Light," "L.A.," "Homecoming," "Lament," "Driving Home at Night with My Children After Their Grandfather's Funeral," "These Days," "Suburban Dusk," *from* "Postcards," "The Poets," "With Animals"

Thanks to Garrett Hongo for letting us reprint "Cello," excerpted from *Volcano: A Memoir of Hawai'i*. Vintage Books, 1996.

BERT MEYERS, A BIBLIOGRAPHY

Books:

Early Rain (Alan Swallow, 1960)

The Dark Birds (Doubleday, 1968)

Sunlight on the Wall (kayak, 1976)

The Wild Olive Tree (West Coast Poetry Review, 1979)

Windowsills (The Common Table, 1979)

The Wild Olive Tree & The Blue Café (JAZZ/BACHY, 1981)

In a Dybbuk's Raincoat: Collected Poems (Morton Marcus and Daniel Meyers, editors. University of New Mexico Press, 2007)

Poems in the following anthologies:

The Birds and the Beasts Were there, ed. William Cole (World, 1963)

Elleve Moderne Amerikanske Lyrikere, ed. Erick Thygesen (Sirius: Odense, Denmark, 1964)

Eight Lines and Under, ed. William Cole (Macmillan, 1967)

Poésie '68, ed. Maison de Culture de Grenoble, France 1968

Just What the Country Needs, Another Poetry Anthology, ed. McMichael and Saleh (Wadsworth, 1971)

Poetry Brief, ed. William Cole (Macmillan, 1971)

Messages, ed. X.J. Kennedy (Little, Brown, 1972)

Poets West, ed. Lawrence Spingarn (Perivale Press, 1975)

The Surrealist Poem in English, ed. Edward Germain (Penguin, 1978)

Voices Within the Ark, the modern Jewish Poets, ed. Howard Schwartz and Anthony Rudolp (Avon 1980)

New Directions Yearly Anthology, ed. James Laughlin (New Directions, 1981)

Anthologie de la Poésie Juive du monde entier depuis les temps bibliques jusqu'à nos jours, ed. Pierre Haiat (Mazarine, 1985)

Inspired by Drink, an anthology, ed. Joan & John Digby (William Morrow & Co., Inc. 1988)

Without a Single Answer, Poems on Contemporary Israel, ed. Elaine Marcus Starkman & Leah Schweitzer (Judah Magnes Museum, 1990)

Wingbeats: Exercises & Practice in Poetry (Dos Gatos Press, 2011.)

BERT MEYERS

BIOGRAPHY:

• born in Los Angeles March 20, 1928

• dropped out of high school, deciding to become a poet

• worked full or part-time at a number of manual jobs, including as a janitor, a carpenter's apprentice, a worker at an airplane factory, and eventually for many years as a picture-framer and gilder in art galleries on La Cienega Blvd. in Los Angeles.

• in 1964, he moved to Claremont, CA., with his wife Odette and children Anat and Daniel. Although he had not gone to undergraduate school, he was exceptionally admitted to the Claremont Graduate School on the basis of his poetry . By 1967, he had completed all his work for a Ph.D. in English literature except for the dissertation and was hired to teach at Pitzer College where he taught poetry workshops, English and American poetry, Russian Literature in translation and Yiddish Literature in Translation, through 1978.

• died April 22, 1979 in Claremont.

PUBLICATIONS:

Books:

Early Rain (Alan Swallow, 1960)
The Dark Birds (Doubleday, 1968)
Sunlight on the Wall (kayak, 1976)
The Wild Olive Tree (West Coast Poetry Review, 1979)
Windowsills (The Common Table, 1979)
The Wild Olive Tree & The Blue Café (JAZZ/BACHY, 1981)

Poems in the following anthologies:

The Birds and the Beasts Were there, ed. William Cole (World, 1963)
Elleve Moderne Amerikanske Lyrikere, ed. Erick Thygesen (Sirius: Odense, Denmark, 1964)
Eight Lines and Under, ed. William Cole (Macmillan, 1967)
Poésie '68, ed. Maison de Culture de Grenoble, France 1968
Just What the Country Needs, Another Poetry Anthology, ed. Mc Michael and Saleh (Wadsworth, 1971)
Poetry Brief, ed. William Cole (Macmillan, 1971)

Bio and bibliography found among Bert's papers.

Messages. ed. X.J. Kennedy (Little, Brown, 1972)
Poets West, ed. Lawrence Spingarn (Perivale Press, 1975)
The Surrealist Poem in English, ed. Edward Germain
(Penguin, 1978)
Voices Within the Ark, the modern Jewish Poets, ed. Howard
Schwartz an Anthony Rudolp (Avon 1980)
New Directions Yearly Anthology, ed. John Laughlin (New
Directions, 1981[?])
Anthologie de la Poésie Juive du monde entier depuis les
temps bibliques jusqu'à nos jours, ed. Pierre Haiat
(Mazarine, 1985)
Inspired by Drink, an anthology, ed. Joan & John Digby
(William Morrow & Co., Inc. 1988)
Without a Single Answer, Poems on Contemporary Israel,
ed. Elaine Marcus Starkman & Leah Schweitzer
(Judah Magnes Museum, 1990)

I was born in Los Angeles, where I lived most of my life. After high school, I worked for seventeen years at various kinds of manual labor, including more than ten years as a picture framer and gilder. Since 1967, I've been an English teacher at Pitzer College in Claremont. I'm married and have two children. I've published ~~two~~ three books of poetry: _Early Rain_ and _The Dark Birds_; and, with my wife, a translation ~~of~~ from the French ~~poet~~ of François Dodat, called _Lord of the Village_. ~~I've received two Ingram Merrill awards and a Na~~ A third book of my own work will be ~~appear~~ published soon. I've received two Ingram Merrill awards and a National Endowment in the Arts grant. My poems often appear in _Kayak_.* | I used to think poetry could change the world. I began with Whitman and Brecht. Now, I prefer ~~Dickinson~~ Baudelaire and Issa; and, I think the last stanza of "Mary Had a Little Lamb" is of far more value to mankind than ~~the entire~~ Pound's entire _Cantos_.

Bert Meyers

* and the West Coast Poetry Review. | and live

Bert's handwritten biography.

“my face was made / to shine among the others.”—from “And Still.”

THIS EDITION OF THE UNSUNG MASTERS
IS PRODUCED AS A COLLABORATION AMONG:

Gulf Coast: A Journal of Literature and Fine Arts
and
Copper Nickel
and
Pleiades: Literature in Context

GENEROUS SUPPORT AND FUNDING PROVIDED BY:

The Nancy Luton Fund
University of Houston Department of English

This book is set in Marion with Avenir
essay titles and Poiret One page numbers.